YOU BET YOUR LIFE

A TOOLBOX FOR

MAKING LIFE'S

ULTIMATE DECISION

PAUL ERNST

Copyright

Unless otherwise indicated, all scripture quotations are taken from the *Holy Bible, New Living Translation*, ©1996. Used by permission of Tyndale House Publishers, Inc., Wheaton, Illinois 60196. All rights reserved. The modern language of the *New Living Translation* is easier for those not practiced in reading scripture and it captures original intent quite well.

TABLE OF CONTENTS

● ● ●

Part IV. Objections to a Christian View of God

Dedication

For Mary, my wife and best friend.

For reminding me when I'm a bit too impressed with myself, that anything worthwhile I might do is from God, so give him the glory. For holding me accountable when I give in to selfishness, pride, and not letting go of the small stuff. For always being there for the big stuff.

Acknowledgements

● ● ●

We all stand on someone's shoulders. One such set of shoulders I have stood on is the community of academics—here I mainly mean Christian and other theistic scholars who have often labored without the credit due their skill and acumen. Sadly they are often under-appreciated by fellow Christians and their work often remains unnoticed except for the few Christians who make it their business to dig down into the foundations for their beliefs.

This book also would not have been possible without the popularizers of Christian thought like California attorney Thomas Anderson, who helped me start my journey when he sent me his thirty-page "legal brief" which eventually became the book *The Verdict*. Another popularizer was Lee Strobel, whose best-selling book The *Case for Christ* made me realize I had to explore the question of Jesus to the fullest understanding I could muster.

Other folks, like Dr. Max Sotak, helped me connect the evidence from books like *The Case for Christ* into a larger system of integrated thought. He pointed me to thinkers like Dr. William Lane Craig, Dr. William Dembsky and Dr. Francis Schaeffer, who possessed the tools to meet difficult challenges in contemporary thought.My first attempt to put my thoughts into writing was met with an underwhelming response. But my friend Steve Laufmann told me that I had something valuable to offer—something that needed to be heard. Through the process Steve would say that what I wrote, "…didn't make sense, you haven't made your case…do it again." His steady perseverance added to mine helped to bring about the completion of this project.

Cathryn Hazouri, in the spirit of friendship, offered to be another set of eyes in reading this document before publication. Her abilities in grammar and syntax enabled me to present this for publishing as a relatively clean manuscript.

My friend Bruce Hibbert volunteered a final reading that caught some mistakes that would have slipped through. He accomplished this in minimal time while preparing the images for the various cosmologies from my hand drawings and notes.

FOREWORD

● ● ●

This book, I'm convinced, is worth your consideration because Paul Ernst's words pierce the deep desires of the ultimate question: What happens when I die? Paul makes the case that Christianity is the answer, and this book is a great read for those who want to understand the evidence.

An explosion of information characterizes our age. Our world is filled with ideas, philosophies, religions, and concepts that often compete or collide. Currently, I serve as a Christian pastor in a city with an influential secular university and a large population base of people who dabble in various New Age and Eastern spiritualities. As a pastor, I often encounter some of the most interesting questions and hypothetical assumptions, along with religious programming that begs a very challenging question: "What is ultimate reality all about?" Those who are seeking to know the unfiltered truth of reality oftentimes do not adequately receive traditional Christian-based answers.

Paul engages this challenge with rigor. He comes from a science background and tends to think like a skeptic. But more importantly he is an everyday person who is passionate about pursuing truth. He begins his discussion with an undeniable point of origin: Something happens when you die! Then lays down this gauntlet:

It should therefore be a high priority for everyone to secure the best possible outcome. Like the voice of Blaise Pascal, the seventeenth century French philosopher, mathematician, and physicist, Paul urges his readers not to be reckless with their souls.

The book walks even the most skeptical readers through a historical pathway that challenges them to consider if their present faith commitment—whether consciously acknowledged or not—is secure. Along this journey, readers will be challenged with the various philosophical worldviews to help them determine if they have latched upon a particular worldview or an irrational combination of potential views that will impact how they will process the evidence.

To evaluate if you have been reckless you must consider these questions: One, what do you believe? Two, why do you believe what you believe? Three, to where does your ultimate destination point? No matter where you are on the worldview map, Paul offers a cumulative case for the Christian worldview. As a researcher, he proposes historical, philosophical, and scientific evidence. As a passionate pursuer of truth, he exposes circular arguments, contradictions that collide, and leaps of oversimplified faith. Paul defends the Bible as both reliable and inspired by looking at its internal evidence and points of correspondence with actual history. He goes after media-hype and misinformation to bolster the authentic case for Christ. This is done with verified details and documentation from recognized scholars.

Paul deals with mammoth objections to the Christian faith, such as the problem of evil. He also deals with the claim that a single way to God is intolerant and provides answers for those who want to know why this supposed true God does not make himself more clearly known.

What separates this book from others that offer answers to what happens when we die is its rigorous analysis compared to the human heart making choices based on desires. Paul shares his journey from doubt to grace and shows how God's free gift is both assuring and threatening because one can never repay what is freely given.

Finally, the reader is shown God's plan to accept his gift of eternal life.

Rev. Douglas R. White
Master of Divinity

Introduction

● ● ●

Albert Einstein said the most remarkable thing about the universe was that it was intelligible. What he meant was that it was open to investigation and accessible to our reason. Why this should be so was a profound mystery to him. Why should mathematics, a product of the human mind, conform exactly to the operations of the physical world? Einstein was smart enough to know that the modern answer, "We evolved to think that way," was inadequate.

I suppose I had asked the usual questions over my life, like where did the universe come from and what will happen when I die? Since I came from a science background, I looked there for answers and found none—just more questions, like the peeling of an onion. I supposed that none existed and so concluded that one must get about the business of life, which consisted of trying to have fun and minimize pain. I knew it was possible that God existed and if I ever encountered him and had to give an account for my unbelief, I was prepared to defend myself with, "Not enough evidence."

Without knowing it, I had uncritically bought into a philosophical system. I had no idea that there was an alternative between taking the world as a brute fact versus blind religious faith, which my rationality and pride would not permit. I had been raised in a minimally Christian home and it never occurred to me to ask if it were true. One day, probably in high school, I decided it wasn't true. I had enough philosophical instinct to be interested in the big questions. But why bother with religion? After all, it's just guessing. Science seemed much more promising, and besides, that's what the smart people did.

Twelve years ago one of the country's top trial lawyers presented me with a paper written as a legal brief defending the deity of Christ.[1] The information it contained went way beyond what I had ever heard in Sunday school or for that matter anywhere else. All this material was sourced and in conformity with a legal standard of evidence. I had no idea if the conclusion was true but for the first time I saw that extraordinary questions could be examined by ordinary means. It might be possible to know something about the claims of Christianity by means other than a blind leap.

I was over fifty and the realization that I was not going to live forever was looming ever larger. I now had some tools in my hands and I was determined to use them. The next eighteen months were a bumpy ride as I drilled through the layers of argument and counter argument. I'll just say at some point I was compelled to believe that Jesus is who he says he is.

Over the next ten years I was driven to know more and to teach others as I learned. I realize that some of my early investigations were done with no background and a bit of naiveté. More study led me to see that some things are not as simple as I first thought. I've had to rework some of my thinking, and I'm not done yet.

---

1   See: Thomas T. Anderson (2008), *Verdict.* Mustang, OK. Tate Publishing

However I'm confident in whom I have put my trust. My desire is to present you with what I have learned as a "tool box." Even if you do not accept my conclusion, I hope you will be better informed in whatever decision you make.

It will be obvious I am not an accomplished writer and I'm not an expert in any of the fields covered here. There is much information on each topic and I encourage you to seek it out. Just be aware that no one is neutral, especially in regards to making ultimate commitments. The quality of discourse is highly variable on all sides. This book is my own synthesis of some of the best thinking on these matters. It's reflective of the way I think. I have been careful to use recognized sources that have been professionally researched. Some of you who will read this know me and it is written with you and your benefit in mind. Some of the wording is in direct response to things you have told me so it may seem intensely personal and perhaps a bit confrontational. I believe the comments you have all made to me regarding faith issues over the years are reflective of the way most people are thinking. I thank my friends for this "window" and hope it will be helpful to others. If you are suffering through this rather dense treatment as a courtesy to me, I thank you in advance. Even if it's just to see what sort of process I went through to form these beliefs, I thank you for that too. I hope your perseverance will be rewarded in some way.

PART I

HOW ARE WE TO THINK ABOUT THE WAY THINGS ARE?

WHY BOTHER WITH THE QUESTION OF ETERNITY?

● ● ●

I n the first century AD when St. Paul went to Athens (Acts 17) to proclaim the divinity of Christ (the unknown God) to the Greek philosophers of his day, some scoffed, some were willing to hear more, and a few accepted his message. The Greco-Roman world was not that different from the modern and postmodern world of today, for there were three prevailing schools of thought, or ways of viewing the world, that could be classified as Epicurean, Stoic, and God-Fearers. Since that time, societies across the world have come into contact with each other, and technologies have changed enormously. Yet the same philosophical themes can be found. In fact, from the beginning of human history until now, all worldviews fall generally into one of three categories: Naturalism, Pantheism, and classical Theism.

Although I will give detailed analysis of these major worldviews in a later chapter, for now I want to suggest that everyone reading this holds to one of these belief systems—either consciously or unconsciously, critically or uncritically. However, because the choice of one's worldview has implications for now and forever, shouldn't this all-important choice be made both consciously and critically?

My goal is to give each of you a tool kit for answering life's biggest questions. This exercise is worth doing. Socrates said, "…

The unexamined life is not worth living…"[2] This exercise should be helpful in clarifying what you believe and why you believe it. Further, you will be prepared to live out your choice knowing what that choice entails.

Before we begin, I must present a cautionary note. None of us makes these monumental decisions in a vacuum. We are products of nature and nurture, family, friends, and societal influence, and the history of ideas that have preceded us. This much is generally recognized. What is less appreciated is that the history of ideas, even if we know or care little about philosophy, is in the air we breathe. Unless you have a background in the history of philosophy, you may have no inkling how much you may be influenced by some past idea that has been filtered through some modern religious or cultural medium. While we would like to believe that our choice of worldview is made through rational objectivity or observing the world as it appears to us, our personal desires exert a powerful influence on our belief-forming process. Whether reading *Scientific American* or watching Oprah, you may be taking in ideas without much examination and with little idea about the assumptions behind their grounding philosophy.

In current Western culture, most are not conditioned to think of religious claims as either true or false. Rather, we are accustomed to viewing them as a matter of preference, not unlike ice cream— you like chocolate, and I like vanilla. Within this framework, to argue about which religion is better (or even true!) seems foolish.

---

2 Plato, *Plato: Complete Works,* trans. J. Cooper and D. Hutchinson (Indianapolis: Hackett, 2005), 33.

But if you are a diabetic, the choice between ice cream and insulin is serious! And the reality is that the true nature of reality has eternal and inescapable consequences. So we should consider our worldview carefully. This decision is not just a choice of ice cream flavors. Think about it in terms of ice cream vs. insulin for a diabetic. We are all diabetics. We have a terminal disease called life.

It is also popular to attempt to maintain that one has no beliefs at all. This is called "agnosticism." "Gnostic" is derived from the Greek infinitive for "to know" (*gnosis*). The "*a*" means *not*, so an agnostic is "one who does not know."

Practically speaking, the idea of not deciding one's worldview, how things *really* are, may sound sensible and open-minded. But the reality is that *something is true*. And it is true whether we know it or not. Though an agnostic stance can be viable when applied to other subjects (such as whether or not you believe in aliens), it is a poor position when it comes to deciding one's worldview. Holding a worldview is a "forced" decision. We face forced decisions all the time: to marry, have children, save for retirement, or vote on a capital case while serving on a jury. Deciding you *don't* believe in God, or an Eastern religion, or the tooth fairy means you have formed some belief. You do have a worldview if only by virtue of what you don't believe. Non-belief is not an option, even if you only believe in yourself.

If you consider yourself an agnostic and have not made a decision about your worldview, I suggest that you take a look at what the various worldviews consist of. Perhaps there is something you can believe in and there is a roadmap for making an informed choice about the most important decision. Why is it most important? For me the answer is self-evident, but I am amazed by the number of people who say they don't care. But what if there were a possibility of being united with your loved ones? Of having a body free of infirmities in a world without death and decay? A world where everyone is in perfect harmony with each other and more importantly with the perfect being that made you, knows you, and is now in perfect relationship with you? Wouldn't you be remiss if there was a roadmap to such an outcome and you didn't bother to look? In comparison, would you choose non-existence or eternal regret? Many reply, "But no one knows for sure." All I am suggesting is that perhaps there is a way to know. Perhaps there is more justification for some beliefs than others. The possibility that you may still get it wrong is not rational grounds for ignoring the matter.

This book is divided into sections. The first will explore our non-rational behavior towards belief forming and how we build our worldviews. The second will present the evidence for the truth of Christianity and how conclusions are drawn from the data. The third will cover common objections and barriers to the Christian faith. Finally, the fourth will look at the implementation of Christianity—if Christianity seems plausible, it should be much more than just an empty set of beliefs about someone named Jesus. So if we decide Christianity is true, what do we do with that decision?

While this book is meant to have a logical progression, some of you may have one big issue that is important to you and little interest in others. It is fine if you skim to that point and concentrate on what interests you most. I realize that for some, the so-called cosmological argument may seem overly abstract, but others who think the current explanations in *Scientific American* or even *Newsweek* make God obsolete may want to pay close attention to the cosmological argument, along with the design argument. On the other hand, if you already believe in God but have doubts concerning Christian claims about Jesus, the chapters on the historical Jesus, New Testament reliability, and the resurrection may be your immediate focus.

Discovering a coherent belief system requires systematic thought. This is where philosophy comes into play. Philosophy can be useful in maintaining consistency and exposing faulty thinking; it can help you identify the assumptions that we all make. The chapter about what makes up a worldview is vital if you don't have the formal skills to do this.

As we shall see, the main choices regarding worldviews are rather few. The multiplicity of philosophies and religions can be reduced to just a few conceptual themes, so there is real hope for believing in something and have a plausible justification for those beliefs.

I am well aware that committing to a conceptual scheme or worldview is not in vogue. It is apparent in most of my conversations that folks prefer just to keep everything up in the air. This state of flux appeals to a culture that does not wish to commit to anything. The more options the better: more freedom, more tolerance, more everything, or so it would seem. We may sense the cost of this freedom. Some of us may wish for solid ground but it just doesn't seem possible with the explosion of information and viewpoints. Over five hundred years before St. Paul gave his speech to the philosophers of Athens, the pre-Socratics were arguing about "being" versus "becoming." The "being" camp (Parmenides) seemed to have logical problems with a world that changes, so the "becoming" camp (Heraclitus) concluded that everything is in a state of constant flux. This idea led to the conclusion that objective knowledge of a thing as it is, is impossible. And this led philosophers from the seventeenth century forward to say we only have access to appearances. Thus we have a distinction between the world as it *appears* to common-sense perception and the world as it *really* is. As Protagoras famously said, "Man is the measure of all things."[3] The similarity with this idea and the secular/progressive/humanist movement of the last 150 years should be apparent. The information explosion and the global village may contribute to this, but there is nothing new under the sun. The old ideas just get recycled.

In an article addressing this, philosopher Peter Kreeft wrote:

The typically modern mind is 1) skeptical of absolutes, unchanging standards and 2) in love with the idea of progress. But this is a logical impossibility, a self-contradiction. Without an unchanging standard, there can be no progress, only change. [4]

---

3   W. T. Jones, *A History of Western Philosophy*. 2ⁿᵈ ed. vol. I, (New York: Harcourt, Brace and World, 1969), 67.

4   P. Kreeft, "Progressivism: The Snobbery of Chronology," *Patheos*. Retrieved from http://www.patheos.com/resources/additional-resorces/progressivism-the-snobbery-of-chronology.html

So applying the idea that man is the measure, you can see the immediate effect on the third branch of philosophy (after Metaphysics and Epistemology) known as *Ethics*. If man is the measure of all things, who decides what is right? The idea that ethics is person, group, or situation relative is well known today, and generally assumed. *Right* has become an individual concept, or one worked out by the *polis* (Greek for city). Functionally, this works out to "What me and my friends think."

I have given this brief and inadequate discourse on early Greek thought to show how captive we are to the past. In the last month I have had three people—all really nice folks—tell me it is not possible to categorically state that torturing babies for fun is always objectively wrong. In a few generations we have abandoned one set of ancient assumptions for another that appears new but isn't.

A few hundred miles east of Athens something else was going on. The Hebrews, with no formal philosophical tradition, held beliefs that could answer the questions the Greeks were wrestling with. Questions like: Where did the world come from? How do I know truth? How am I supposed to live? They had the answers because the Creator of the world had revealed them. The reason that what God had revealed to them was intelligible, while the Greeks were mired in paradox, is because God made the recipients of his revelation in his image, so a rational (verbal) communication from the Creator to the creature was possible.

At this point I am not asking you to believe this is the case. That is to be established. All I am suggesting is that if man is to be more than his illusions and delusions, a scheme like that of the Hebrews, based on an absolute personal Creator distinct from creatures that bear his image, is a necessary condition for existence, knowledge, and ethics.

I am saying that without a God like the Hebrews had—an infinite personal God who "speaks" to his creatures—man lacks a basis for explaining the existence of the world, for providing a basis for knowing things truly, and for knowing what is required of him in his dealings with man and God. To this, some might say: "Good, I like everything up for grabs. I don't care if the big questions have answers or not, and if I do, I'll make up my own, thank you." All I can suggest at this point is that you might be better off with a level of certitude and invite you to take a look at an old idea in some ways that you perhaps never thought of.

As an important part of our search for truth, we will look at historical and scientific evidence that can be used to justify a worldview. The choice of the types of evidence you may be willing to consider depends on your prior intellectual or emotional commitments, so your choice is ultimately grounded in faith—namely that in which you put your trust. We all trust something. The question is: have you evaluated *why* you trust what you do? The Naturalist trusts his or her *physical senses* to evaluate what is out there. Far Eastern religion (Pantheism) values *mystical intuition*. We all make faith commitments, but that does not mean they have equal coherence or explanatory power. In other words, some faith commitments are better than others.

In this book I'll present arguments for: 1) a supernatural (outside of nature) personal cause of the universe, 2) evidence of purposeful design in nature, 3) the existence of objective moral values (hence an objective and transcendent source of values), and 4) a case for the supernatural origin of the Hebrew/Christian Bible, including the historical basis for the resurrection of Jesus.

Though each of these arguments can be doubted, I hope to persuade the reader that they have some force and are worthy of consideration. As I wrestled with these ideas in my search for truth—from the origin of the universe to the reliability of the Bible—I got caught up in a morass of counterarguments and even counters to those. This appeared to be leading to a kind of global skepticism. But as I continued, a pattern emerged. There were only so many ways you could slice this stuff. Either one side fell away due to an accumulation of evidence, or a decision could be made on the basis of a simple presupposition—such as the possibility that a being like the God of the Bible *could* exist.

The point is not to provide absolute proof (which is not possible in endeavors other than formal logic), but that Christianity is a more plausible account of the creation—of man and his condition—than the alternatives are. My intent is to show that there is rational warrant for anyone who is willing to accept that Christianity could be true. And truth (as the key to what is "the good" as the Greeks might have called it) should be believed.

I admit that the very nature of this material is dogmatic. And I say this without apology, since everyone—even the most "Zen" among us—is committed to some kind of dogma.

I also hope to do this with some humility. As a Christian, I believe in absolute truth, but at the same time I realize that I am finite and capable of error. Our desires to justify our own actions and beliefs have worked their way into our ability to see and reason about the way the world truly is. Both Christians and non-Christians have this problem. Even St. Paul said, "We see through the glass darkly."[5]

---

5   1 Corinthians 13:12 (KJV).

We All Have Skin in the Game

● ● ●

L ast year at the gym, a retired college professor was trying to get me more concerned about global warming. Global warming is one of those subjects that seems (to me) to be more about politics than science, and I am a bit skeptical. I finally explained to the professor that if he wanted to win me over, he would have to do more than call me an idiot and proclaim that the issue had already been decided, and that the science was "settled." Anytime someone tells me something is "settled," I view it with suspicion.

Knowing this was going nowhere, he decided to try another approach. He explained to me that even if I thought the chances of human-caused global warming were small, the worst-case scenario was so catastrophic that a prudent person would take it seriously. I agreed with his point. He then went on to explain that humans do a lousy job of assessing risk. He made comparisons between not wearing a seat belt (significant) and worrying about asteroid strikes (not). Again, I agreed with him. Since he had already cued up the ball for me, I asked him if he knew about Pascal's wager regarding belief in God:

Yes, but you must wager. There is no choice, you are already committed. Which will you choose then? Let us see which offers you the least interest. You have two things to lose: the true and

> the good; and two things to stake: your reason and happiness; and your nature has two things to avoid: error and wretchedness. Since you must necessarily choose, your reason is no more affronted by choosing one rather than the other. That is one point cleared up. But your happiness? Let us weigh up the gain and the loss involved in calling heads that God exists. Let us assess the two cases: if you win, you win everything; if you lose, you lose nothing. Do not hesitate then; wager that he does exist.[6]

If we bet on the Christian God and we are right, we gain an infinite good. However, if we are wrong, we have lost nothing. On the other hand, if we bet against God and we are wrong, we have an infinite loss. If we bet against God and we are right, we gain nothing. So the Atheist/Agnostic is in a lose/lose situation. My friend, as an educated man, knew this famous argument. In this context, I asked him if he could name the greatest personal threat he could ever personally face. Was it global warming, a brain tumor, or possible divine judgment after death? He seemed numbed by the question. He was utterly incapable of applying this simple "decision matrix" to life's biggest question while he used it deftly on far less serious matters.

Blaise Pascal was a wealthy Frenchman enjoying the pleasures of seventeenth century Paris. He later underwent a mystical conversion experience and renounced the pleasures of the flesh for a godly life. At his core, however, Pascal was no mystic. He had reasoned carefully from the scriptures to show that the Bible has an internal system of prophecy and fulfillment that supported its

---

6   B. Pascal, *Penses*, trans. A. J. Krailsheimer, (New York: Penguin, 1995), 123.

claims of supernatural origin. For example, in comparing the Bible to the Koran, Pascal said the following:

> It is not the same with scripture. I admit [in the scriptures] that there are obscurities as odd as those of Mahomet [Mohammed], but some things are admirably clear, with [the] prophecies manifestly fulfilled. So [between the Bible and Koran] it is not an even contest.[7]

By reasoning from the scriptures, Pascal rooted his faith in Christ. Pascal's contemporaries noticed the change in his life but were unwilling to consider his arguments in favor of Christianity. Aware that his contemporaries were not interested in what God had to say, Pascal framed his famous wager as a way to get them to think about the issue at hand: eternal destiny.

Put simply, the wager encourages eternal risk assessment. The wager holds that even if a person is not sure whether God exists, it is better to wager (to live life or "bet") as though God does exist because one has everything to gain (going to heaven and escaping hell). However, if God does not exist, only oblivion awaits after death. Non-existence of the self is the outcome either under Naturalism or Eastern (pantheistic) religions.

Douglas Goothuis writing in Pascal's voice wrote:

> As gamblers...they understand stakes and odds and outcomes. They also understand...that some choices are 'momentous' and 'forced.' To not believe in God may have momentous negative consequences, while believing in God may have momentous positive consequences for this life and in the life to come. Moreover,

---

7   B. Pascal, *Penses*, trans. A. J. Krailsheimer, (New York: Penguin, 1995), 45.

the situation is forced in that time is running out. One must ultimately take a stand for or against the Christian claim on reality.[8]

Avoiding the issue by remaining skeptical is not an option. We cannot avoid the issue because, as William James (a non-Christian) put it, "If religion be true and the evidence for it be still insufficient, I do not wish…to forfeit my sole chance in life of getting upon the winning side…"[9] Though Pascal's gamblers can see that the stakes are high and that they must wager, they are not guaranteed in their choice, but how will we choose?

The argument in the wager is not so naïve as to claim that people can choose to believe in a particular worldview as easily as they can use their willpower to raise their hands. Even a man who is dying can still complain that he cannot force himself to believe in God, because he is already convinced that the evidence for God's existence is lacking.

While Pascal urges that we decide to have faith in God on the basis of "prudential outcomes"—the heart of the wager, namely heaven and hell—and that it makes sense for the dying man to believe, the fact is that a skeptical dying man *cannot just make himself* trust in Jesus Christ as his Lord and Savior.

Pascal's advice to a person in such a situation, or preferably long before it, is that he or she attempt to still or allay their "passion for unbelief." How does one accomplish this? The retarding of the passion for unbelief may come about through faith-forming religious

---

8   D. Groothuis "Pascal Speaks from the Grave," *Think,* (Autumn, 2004): 49-50.

9   W. James, *The Will to Believe*, (Harvard, 1896), http://educ.jmv.edu/~omerawm/ph101willtobelieve.html

activities. Pascal is not recommending liturgical brainwashing! Rather, he observes that our belief-forming processes are affected by our passions, as well as by reason. In some cases, our passions can be somewhat abated through certain courses of action taken over time.[10]

But while Pascal advises "religious activity" to his generation (to overcome doubts about faith in Christ); the situation for today's postmodern skeptic is more difficult. Arguments from science, philosophy, and historical criticism of the scriptures (and a general disdain from the elite) would seem to place a heavy burden against belief in the claims of Christianity. However, I will argue in later chapters that the force of these objections has been severely undercut by modern Christian scholarship. It has been argued that now is the best time in the last one hundred years to believe in God.

I would like to suggest that the root of your unbelief may not be so much that you have carefully evaluated the evidence for and against Christianity, but it is likely that you are a product of your upbringing (or reacting against it). This could be because of your education (peer pressure from friends and colleagues), or selection bias in your consumption of media, or some other combination of social factors. A big barrier to faith is the sheer amount of (dis)information, especially with the Internet and five hundred cable channels. This breeds skepticism and reduces the chance that the truth can break through the clutter.

---

10 The connotation of "passions" in this context is not entirely sexual. It could be power, material possessions, a political viewpoint, or anything you strongly desire that is not compatible with following God. In this context, even the "good" can become bad.

The will to believe comes from an active mind that seeks truth. My hope is that through a proper application of the wager, you will attain the will to cut through the controlling beliefs of your past and take an honest, open-minded look at the evidence.

With that said, no matter how attractive the Christian outcome is, I understand that the heart cannot rejoice in what the mind rebels against. I hope the evidence section of this book will help free you of this burden. And if you find this dubious right now, I completely understand.

Personally, I have always liked the Christian story, but during my skeptical days (ages 13-52) I found it incredible, almost like Santa Claus. In some sense, I had the desire (but not the will) to believe, but I felt a greater need not to violate what I thought was a commitment to rational thought. At least I had convinced myself that I was committed to rational thought. As I look back, that was a bit of a hoot, as I was not really committed to anything but myself. At the time, little did I understand that only God could be the foundation for the very concept of reason. If there is no God, we humans are nothing more than advanced deterministically programmed, tool making apes. We may have survival abilities, but there is no possibility that a random collocation of atoms will produce anything like rational thought, except in the sense of a chess-playing computer. Atheist philosopher, Daniel Dennit, states that we have competence without comprehension. So as I imagined I was exercising my rational mind, unbeknownst to me, I was affirming God's existence.

One final comment about the wager: it has its critics among Christians and non-Christians alike.

Christians correctly point out that thinking just in terms of the wager is nothing like having real trust in God. Intellectual agreement is a necessary but not a sufficient condition of genuine trust. Further, Christianity uniquely claims that salvation cannot be attained through human effort—good works, meditations, self-realization, etc. Used by itself, applying the wager (in terms of faith and religious activities) is an attempt at some sort of fire insurance. Again this is not the same as trust in a person.

Non-Christians correctly point out that the wager is not a proof for the existence of God. Dr. Alan Carter, a scholar and skeptic philosopher along the lines of David Hume, in a debate with Dr. Doug Groothuis at the University of Colorado, said that the wager failed because it failed to specify *which* God. It might even be a deal with the Devil; or perhaps a malicious God that would turn the tables and condemn those who believe in him and save those who do not. But Pascal was quite clear that the weight of the evidence left little room for other gods. He plainly did not see any other live options among the world's religions. The coming sections on worldviews and Christian evidences will offer reasons that may help you come to share Pascal's confidence. In the meantime, the wager's purpose is to shake us out of our dogmatic slumber and realize that we all have skin in the game.

WHO BEARS THE BURDEN?

● ● ●

A well-known debate tactic is to try to get one's opponent to bear the burden of proof. Another way of putting this is to say that the one who makes the claim bears the burden. In the criminal justice system, suspects are innocent until proven guilty. The prosecution must prove that the claim of guilt is "beyond a reasonable doubt." Failing that, innocence will be the default verdict. In a civil case the standard is lower and calls for the "preponderance of the evidence." Sometimes philosophers will just settle for a proposition to "be more plausible than its denial." In that case, you have warrant or justification to believe it. Of course, that doesn't mean you have to. But if the matter involves a really important decision, a forced decision like in the wager, then there would seem to be an even greater reason to go with the "best outcome" rather than quibbling about small differences in probabilities.

Given that the wager is based on self-interest or "prudential outcomes," the burden of proof would seem to be placed on the non-believer. But at this point the skeptic may raise the so-called "intellectualist objection." For example, if you offer me a thousand dollars to believe the sky is green, I may want the money, but I can't conjure up the belief, no matter how much I may want to. But Pascal is not asking that you believe something manifestly untrue, although Christianity may seem that to one indoctrinated with modernist assumptions. Pascal believed in a system of evidence that proved the Bible is self-authenticating. It makes predictions about future events…and their fulfillments are clearly demonstrated in many cases. Pascal saw this was lacking in other holy books like the Koran. Since Biblical writings are extant (present) today—including copies even closer to the originals than in the Bible available to Pascal, scholars have a permanent record of a supernatural phenomenon that is open to historical investigation. So the skeptic bears the double burden of undercutting the evidence while working against his own self-interest. This is hard to do with the facts on the table, but the new aggressive brand of Atheism relies on the fact that most people don't know the Christian case. If in one's mind Christianity only stands one chance in one hundred or even one chance in ten of being true, then some people—perhaps many—will take the asymmetrical bet against their own best interest. The wager may be a good bet on a coin toss but it may seem like a poor one against lottery-like odds. Even for someone with the will to believe in God, the supposed odds against Theism may cause them to reject faith out of a perceived sense of duty to rational decision-making (or result in a life of faith in God that is plagued with constant doubt—not healthy and not what God intended). This was essentially my position before studying the matter

However, the classic Atheist tactic of shifting the burden of proof cuts both ways.

I once introduced myself as a Christian to an Atheist group with a booth at the Boulder Creek Festival in Boulder, Colorado. All smiles, a man stepped out and said, "Boy, you have a lot of explaining to do!" Then he brought up his list of "implausible" events (miracles) and expected me to tap dance my way through all of his "What about this?" questions. I agreed that his list of doubts was extensive, and that I would be happy to go through some of the details, if he had the time to get past mere caricatures and bumper-sticker anti-religious assertions. Then I pointed out that he was the one who had the most to explain.

"What do you mean"? He replied, "I don't have to explain anything."

"On the contrary," I said. "You must explain the oldest question in philosophy: Why is there something instead of nothing?" The usual Atheist answer is that the universe is a brute fact and no explanation is required.

He subsequently had to admit that Atheism makes strong claims about reality too. The Atheist would like you to think unbelief in a personal God is no different than unbelief in Zeus. My new friend then asked me an honest and substantive question about why Jesus did not return in one generation like he claimed he would in the Bible. This type of question has the possibility of resolution through evidence—real historical documents. I gave him an answer that he found interesting, and while I don't think I changed his mind, I did get him to change his tactics. He knew these questions turned on evidence and he had to produce counter arguments. Naturalism (nature is all there is, a view that is functionally equivalent to Atheism) bears a burden of justification, just like any other worldview.[11]

Another "burden" tactic, used by Carl Sagan in his *Cosmos* series, is to say that extraordinary claims demand extraordinary evidence. He implies that religious claims are utterly extraordinary. He also implies that there is nothing extraordinary about Naturalism at all. Again, Sagan's claims are riddled with intellectual dishonesty and willful bias.

Who is to say that the Christian claims are extraordinary and that the evidence for Christianity is inadequate to support the claim? Christian claims are only extraordinary if one accepts Naturalism as the standard. Without prior knowledge of the facts, how would one know that the supernatural is less plausible than the natural? A mole does not believe in birds because it lacks the proper sight. Likewise, Sagan's telescope is not the proper tool for reaching his conclusion. Sagan's claim that the universe came from nothing seems extraordinary to me.

The Naturalist's answer is that the natural is empirically verifiable (i.e., accessible to the senses), whereas the supernatural is not. But that is exactly the point! Sense experience can only tell us about the natural world, unless of course the supernatural wants to intrude into the natural world in such a way as to make itself known. To demand empirical proof for the supernatural would be like asking someone to weigh a chicken with a yardstick. However, naturalistic empiricists constantly misuse this argument.

---

11 A note on Alvin Plantinga's position. I know there is a strong argument that some beliefs, like the belief in other minds, need no justification. God seems to be one of those "properly basic" beliefs.

Eugenie Scott, executive director of the National Center for Science Education, uses the argument that God is empirically undetectable as her way of ruling God out of court—least with respect to science. While she is correct about direct observation regarding God, she overlooks another form of argument: inference to the best explanation. When previously offered hypotheses fail to explain a given set of facts, and then a new explanation is offered that far exceeds the prior ones in explanatory scope and power (and is the least *ad hoc*), then one is justified in holding to that new explanation—unless some defeater arises. In terms of explaining the existence of the universe, if Christianity best fits the evidence (far better than Naturalism), then it makes sense to believe in Christianity—unless a defeater, like the dead body of Jesus, were found.

Inferring the best explanation is how humans do most of their thinking. This is exactly how forensic and historical sciences work: evidence is gathered, and the most plausible explanation is accepted if it far exceeds its competitors. So when a supernatural cause (in the sense of one outside of nature) is the best explanation of the universe, it is nothing more than bias for Naturalists like Scott to rule out God's existence.

Arguments such as those for the resurrection of Jesus use the inference to the best explanation. This is the appropriate method for reasoning about past events. The historical sciences, which include not just human history but any "look back" science like paleontology and even astronomy must use inference, because the scientific method (observation and experimentation) is not possible for past events and non-repeatable phenomena. Christian evidence at least claims to be historical, so this method of inference should be valid and expected to yield results. To those who claim that miracles are by nature not historical, I say, "Says who?" We will look at the problem of miracles in a later chapter. For now, I will say that the infrequency of miracles is not an argument against them, as the Atheist David Hume asserts. Rather, infrequency is part of the definition of a miracle; otherwise, miracles would be seen as commonplace natural occurrences. Here I am referring to the special miracles that God uses to inform mankind of a specific intent, such as those in the life of Jesus. Another class of God's action in the world is found everywhere and is open to investigation, as we will see in the design argument, which is also based on inference to the best explanation. The inference process requires that *all* explanations must be put on the table, not just those permitted by the person with the microphone.

Another tactic of the skeptic is "upping the ante." This means that no matter how much evidence the Christian produces in favor of Christian Theism, the skeptic will claim that it is simply not enough. So exactly how much evidence does the skeptic need? The constant answer is: "More than you've given me so far." This approach frees the skeptic to walk away saying, "See, you didn't answer *all* of my questions. I have no reason to believe in God." But when this technique is pursued past the point of reasonableness, it becomes a dodge that allows the skeptic to ignore the evidence that has already been given. He feels vindicated without having to grapple with the arguments in favor of Theism. A classic example is the Atheist that demands lighting strike in fifteen minutes and citing this non-event as evidence against God. I suppose if lighting did strike, it would have been ascribed to luck rather than God.

Finally, there is the "leap of faith" objection—the argument that believing in God is nothing more than "blind faith."

Sadly, Christians perpetuate this as much as Atheists. The term originated with the Christian existentialist Soren Kierkegaard. Kierkegaard—at the time when enlightenment rationalism was in full sway and criticism of the Bible was unchallenged—was looking for a way to believe in God through a sort of "will to believe." He was also trying to infuse new life into the spiritually dead Danish state church. Kierkegaard's position was actually far more sophisticated than a mere admonition for others to conjure up faith in Christ, but the term "leap of faith" stuck as a description of his rationale.

But this "leap" concept suffers from an improper use of the word faith. Mark Twain said, "Faith is believing what you know ain't so." In sharp contrast, the Bible appeals to evidence and testing. Biblical trust is trust in eyewitness accounts, written records, and—in the case of the apostles—their own empirical verification. Of course, not everyone accepts the reliability of the historical records, but that is another discussion. While some Christians may do so, Biblical Christianity never asks anyone to take a blind leap into the unknown.

The "leap" also conjures the image of someone who is standing on the solid ground of unbelief jumping off into irrationality due to some psychological need.

To the extent that the arguments we'll develop in this book have merit, then Christianity *is* the solid ground and picking an alternate belief system would, in fact, be the blind leap.

Renowned British (former) Atheist Antony Flew told his Atheist supporters not to use the psychological argument (i.e., that belief is just a projection of our desires) to explain away belief in God because it can cut both ways. The innate desire to be autonomous is strong psychological incentive against belief. We are all subject to our desires all of the time. Critical thinking skills and a keen appreciation for the role of presuppositions in one's thinking is the best defense against the charge of Freudian (or any other kind of) projection.

We live in a world where "religion always bears the burden of proof" arguments are so common that "educated" folks have simply absorbed them. If we blindly accept the idea that Naturalism is the default position, this will become a hidden barrier to our ability to properly consider the evidence and infer the best explanation for the universe's existence, for design in nature, and for specific Christian claims about Jesus.

The point is this: in any contest of ideas, both sides bear a burden of proof or some form of justification, and winning means having the most plausible position, not one that is beyond question.

DEVELOPING A WORLDVIEW

To understand the world of ideas, philosophy, and religion, it is necessary to understand how worldview thinking works.

The following material is based on copyrighted work by Dr. Max H. Sotak. His paper, *Philosophical Disagreements and Worldviews*, is a primer for students of philosophy and religion. Professor Sotak's subspecialty is metaphilosophy, or how philosophical systems are constructed. Much of this material is based on his paper and I wish to give him credit for it, since it has enabled me to understand this complex subject and interact informatively and honestly with various philosophical positions. According to Dr. Sotak:

> For most people, a worldview is a set of control beliefs that determines the way they reason about their experience. Since the way a person reasons about experience is based on underlying commitments, the philosophically naïve person experiences his own views as obvious and self-evident.[12]

All experience is viewed through the preexisting worldview lens. Any hints that another worldview might be true are filtered out (or consciously eliminated). When another person comes to a different conclusion working with the same data, that person is viewed as

---

12   Max H. Sotak, *"Philosophical Disagreements and Worldviews"* (2003), 1.

irrational, or as Richard Dawkins once put it, "...ignorant, stupid, or insane..."[13]

Sotak goes on to explain this in some detail, which I think is useful to quote:

> Since philosophy is a very detailed and complex discipline, beginning students simply lose the forest for the trees and end up combining a potpourri of ideas from various philosophers depending on what resonates with their personal views. Usually this approach leaves the student confused about how theoretical thinking really works and often produces less clarity and more skepticism about the prospect of finding truth in philosophy...[14]
>
> What makes a worldview perspective even more powerful is that it provides insight into why certain principles seem self-evident to a particular philosopher. For example, Thomas Hobbes believed that moral principles are derived from a consideration of pleasure and pain in our experience. Good is equated with pleasure and evil is equated with pain. He did not believe in moral absolutes like Immanuel Kant, nor did he believe that moral absolutes come from God like St. Augustine. Hobbes' view stemmed from his belief that matter is all that exists, a position called Materialism. Since all we sense is matter, there is nothing else from which to derive ethical principles. Notice the kind of circularity in this position. Matter is Hobbs' metaphysical principle—what he believes is *real*, eternal, and self-existent. Sense experience is Hobbes' epistemological principle—how he believes he *knows* what is real and self-existent. And pleasure is Hobbes ethical principle—what he believes is the standard of moral action...

---

13 R. Dawkins,"Put Your Money on Evolution," *New York Times,* April 9, 1989, Section VII, 35.

14 Ibid., 1.

It should be obvious that one's basic metaphysical commitment is really the key to one's entire philosophy. What you believe is ultimately real, eternal and self-existent will determine how you know it and how you derive moral principles. While many philosophers claim neutrality and objectivity when it comes to how they know, the truth is that all philosophy begins with a foundational metaphysical commitment that is not based purely on reason, sense experience, or some combination of the two. Indeed, the foundational commitment determines how reason and sense experience are used in determining truth...

What's more, every thinker is faced with a major problem: how can finite human beings know what is ultimately real without being omniscient? In other words, if I believe that what I see is all that is real, how do I know I am seeing everything there is? Maybe there is something real that I don't see but must be taken into account. So for example, I do not see God, but if God is an invisible spirit, maybe God is really there after all. Deep down, most people realize that there may be real things we simply don't see. After all, who has ever seen a quark or a law of logic?...

In the end, most philosophers resort to some kind of evidence to justify their belief concerning what is ultimately real. Reason, sense experience, intuition and revelation are the main sources of evidence for our beliefs about what ultimately exists. Revelation in nature and sacred scriptures have been considered major sources of knowledge by theists because they point to an omniscient revealer above the world, thus overcoming the "problem of omniscience." Other philosophers will ignore this problem and go with some combination of reason, self-experience and/or intuition—taking the world itself as the starting point. Since human belief and reasoning are affected by personal philosophical likes and dislikes, desire also plays a role in this reckoning. For example, a person who does not want to believe in God will likely slight or ignore any purported evidence counting for such a belief. But whatever evidence is offered to justify a metaphysical ultimate, an element of faith is inescapable. One must *commit* to the reliability of reason, sense experience, revelation, etc., and the reliability of these sources of truth is disputed by one philosopher or another...

What then are the basic worldviews, and how do we account for the philosophical disagreements even within world views? Some philosophers would say there are only three basic world views, each has internal variations: (1) Theism, (2) Pantheism, and (3) Naturalism. Theism is the belief in one personal God that is eternal and self-existing. Being transcendent, or above the world, he is not dependent on the world but is, in fact, its creator. Pantheism is a misleading term because the word *theism* at the heart of the word has personal connotations for most Westerners. This view combines two ideas: All (pan) is God (theism). In this position, there is no personal God above the universe, but rather the universe as a whole *is* God. The difference from theism as a world view is that Pantheism does not affirm belief in a personal God and is, therefore, atheistic. In short, the universe is essentially impersonal. Like Pantheism, Naturalism is also atheistic. Indeed, a spiritual God cannot exist, for there is no spirit in a purely material universe.

Even though every philosophy may be generally classified in terms of three basic world views, it is also necessary to explain the variations among philosophies within the same world view. ...As it turns out, there are two tendencies within atheistic world views. One tendency is reductionistic and the other is personalistic. What this means is that some philosophies attempt to explain the world by reducing it to one or more of its subhuman aspects, while others explain the world primarily in terms of some or all human aspects.[15]

---

15 This long quote has been used by permission from Max H. Sotak, *Philosophical Disagreements and Worldviews* (2003), 1–8.

Most Theists appeal to some form of written revelation but differ according to their sources of revelation and the evidence for them. Most also believe that the natural world, as a created entity, is a form of revelation from God and gives evidence for God's existence. However, most theistic worldviews also indicate that revelation from nature alone is inadequate for sinful man to understand God's requirements, and a more specific knowledge is revealed in various holy scriptures. Judaism accepts this notion and holds that only the Hebrew Bible (Old Testament) is inspired by God. Christianity proclaims that the entire Bible (Old and New Testaments) is the revealed word of God. Islam accepts the above (nature and the Bible as sources), but believes that the final revelation came through the prophet Muhammad and the Koran, because the Bible was "corrupted" by Jews and Christians. If these scriptures contain truths, such as God created the world and man is morally responsible to him, they would help solve the problem of omniscience: finite man's inability to transcend himself and truly know his situation with respect to reality (i.e., things as they really are).

Interestingly, both Theism and Pantheism acknowledge the problem of omniscience and that finite man cannot find ultimate reality unless *it* reveals itself. While not denying that reason and sense experience tell us something about the world, Theists *know* about ultimate things by committing to a revelation from a personal God. Pantheists, while understanding the problem, simply "plug in" (meditate) on an impersonal universe, which will hopefully tell them something through a mystical experience and non-rational intuition.

Figure 1 shows the circularity between *being* and *knowing*—what you believe is ultimately real determines how you know it. The order of epistemic sources in each circle is important.

The Naturalist/Materialist relies principally upon sense experience, and reason is secondary. This is because (according to Naturalism) reason is simply a product of material causes (e.g., biological evolution) and is no guarantor of the process of rational inference, much less ultimate truth. In fact if Naturalism is true, *we lack the grounds* for *knowing that Naturalism is true.* Naturalism undercuts it own justification. Naturalists like Richard Dawkins make much over their free will and their reason. Yet this is a

A WORLD VIEW PERSPECTIVE OF BEING AND KNOWING
What Ultimately Exists (Being) Determines How You Know It (Knowing)

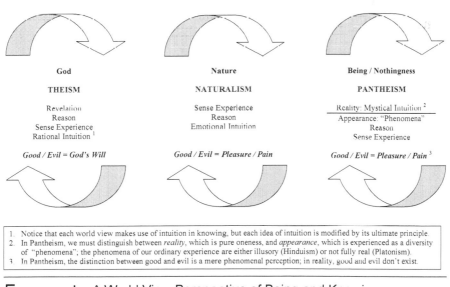

God	Nature	Being / Nothingness
THEISM	**NATURALISM**	**PANTHEISM**
Revelation	Sense Experience	Reality: Mystical Intuition [2]
Reason	Reason	Appearance: "Phenomena"
Sense Experience	Emotional Intuition	Reason
Rational Intuition [1]		Sense Experience
Good / Evil = God's Will	*Good / Evil = Pleasure / Pain*	*Good / Evil = Pleasure / Pain* [3]

1. Notice that each world view makes use of intuition in knowing, but each idea of intuition is modified by its ultimate principle.
2. In Pantheism, we must distinguish between *reality*, which is pure oneness, and *appearance*, which is experienced as a diversity of "phenomena"; the phenomena of our ordinary experience are either illusory (Hinduism) or not fully real (Platonism).
3. In Pantheism, the distinction between good and evil is a mere phenomenal perception; in reality, good and evil don't exist.

FIGURE 1. A World View Perspective of Being and Knowing. *(From Philosophical Disagreements and Worldviews, Max H. Sotak. Used by permission.)*

logical incoherence in their philosophy, as Naturalism supports neither.[16]

In the case of Pantheism, one comes to understand the impersonal "ground of being" principally through mystical intuition. Sense experience is merely phenomenal (an appearance, not ultimately real), and reason is ultimately superseded by mystical experience, even when it violates the laws of reason. The Pantheist does not hold that sense experience corresponds to reality. (Note that the Naturalist says that sense experience does correspond to reality, but it can only point to survival value, which is of limited utility for answering life's big questions.)

Only Theism provides grounds for both sense experience and reason to correspond to reality. This is because God creates a world separate from himself that is in some sense "real." God is a personal spirit, so he can make creatures in his image that possess some of his properties such as personhood. As his image bearers, the way is opened to the knowledge of God.

Most adherents to various worldviews accept the above analysis as a fair representation of their belief systems. However, many philosophers and some Eastern religions reject the whole idea of finding ultimate reality. For them, metaphysics—the search for what is real—is just a word game. Similarly, analytic philosophy (dominant in the last seventy years) despairs of ultimate answers and is resigned to studying how we think about reality and express it as language. Most of the traditional Protestant Christian

16 Victor Reppert, *C. S. Lewis's Dangerous Idea* (Downer's Grove, IL: Inter-Varsity Press, 2003).

denominations have now replaced theology, the study of God, with the study of how people think about God. The religion departments at all secular and many "religious" universities amount to largely sociology or anthropology studies. Finally, Postmodernism, the "spirit of the age," declares any attempt to tell an overarching story is just an attempt at imposing the views of one group on another.

However, all of us have made a worldview commitment somewhere along the line. Even those who reject the idea that they adhere to a particular philosophy always give themselves away by how they live and act. Specifically, most of the "I don't have a religion" or "I'm spiritual" folks would reject Christian Theism. This statement in itself is a claim to know something ultimate about the universe; they allegedly know enough to reject the Christian God.

Whether you are a Pantheist, a Theist, a Naturalist, or someone who claims to be religiously neutral, taking a metaphysical position of some kind (or even denying those positions that you reject) is inescapable. Something is real, and what you reject implies what you affirm. The take-home message is this: you have a worldview, and it affects how you interpret evidence.

Developing and Assessing Evidence

• • •

When I was in the process of investigating the Christian claims, I told my business partner, "It really appears that Jesus was raised from the dead." He said that he did not have a problem with that. To my surprise, he thought that it is probably true and resurrection was just a matter of possessing sufficient enlightenment. Anyone could potentially do the same! That certainly caught me off guard.

Among Christians, it is assumed that Christianity stands or falls on the truth of the resurrection (see 1 Corinthians 15). But here I was confronted with a person who assented to the fact of the resurrection, but was completely unmoved towards any traditional practice of the Christian faith.

The reason was that my friend was committed to the worldview of Eastern Pantheism. Under this belief system, *everything* is god/nature—miracles are a part of nature, a part of the ALL, the undifferentiated oneness of reality. For the Pantheist, this natural world is made of spirit or energy that can be manipulated spiritually, similar to how we work with natural forces like electricity—through techniques using mind and body. Spirit is just another force to be brought under our control, so to my friend the resurrection was no big deal. It showed that Jesus had special knowledge, perhaps learned in India or Egypt! Whoever you may think Jesus is, he has to be explained through the background of first century Judaism. Jesus thought he was the Jewish Messiah and not some Eastern guru.

I recount this to show that facts are often held hostage to one's worldview. Specifically, people have a tendency to first assume that a certain worldview is true and then consciously or subconsciously force the facts to support that worldview. Whether a Naturalist, a Pantheist, or a Theist; each of us must put our trust in *something* so a measure of this circular reasoning is unavoidable. Thus, an element of faith (trust) is required under any belief system, even Naturalism. But this does not mean that all worldviews are equal.

If you are committed to Naturalism, you have faith that through the course of random evolution you somehow evolved a rational freethinking mind and natural senses that allow you to accurately perceive the reality of the natural world. While there may be some strange phenomena in this universe, all evidence pointing to something beyond the material world will be rejected. Case in point: No amount of historical evidence will convince Richard Dawkins (author of *The God Delusion*) that the resurrection actually happened. *Skeptic* magazine's Michael Shermer has demanded a material explanation of how God did it before he will believe it. But Shermer misses the point. If we had a *material* explanation, it wouldn't be Christian evidence!

Likewise, a Pantheist has faith in his or her inner divinity— everything is God, including all humans. A person who believes that everything is God may find the resurrection plausible but not unique—after all, according to Pantheism everyone has the "God consciousness," and Jesus merely realized his to the fullest. However, to move forward with the facts that support the historical case for Christianity and the resurrection; the fundamental assumption (e.g., faith commitment) is that there is a transcendent, personal God who stands distinct from the creation (a.k.a. the universe). To understand the resurrection and its true meaning, one must accept that Naturalism and Pantheism are both false and that the Theistic worldview is true.

If you are already committed to Naturalism or Pantheism, Christian evidences will simply be interpreted through the lens of another worldview. Because of this, I must make the case for the Theistic worldview plausible before I present evidence for Christianity. So it's worthwhile to revisit worldview thinking— I've already claimed that there are only three worldviews, possibly reducible to just two. But can it really be that simple?

There are thousands of belief systems. This makes any claim to have "the one true religion" seem silly or arrogant. Skepticism towards any religious claims of an exclusivist nature seems necessary. But remember that skepticism itself is both a belief system and a truth claim. Yet can skepticism justify itself? Perhaps one should be skeptical of one's own skepticism!

Regardless, if all the thousands of belief systems can be reduced to a few basic categories, then we have the possibility of finding truth even if it is by process of elimination. Before we begin evaluating belief systems, we must first define what they are.

When I have taught this material, I often ask people how many different ideas they can come up with to account for the existence of what they call "reality" or "the universe." Though the phrasing differs from person to person, it generally boils down to these few:

1. **The universe is eternal and self-existent.** This has a long history but has predominated in the post-Enlightenment era. The naturalistic version says that the universe is purely material. The pantheistic version says that the universe is entirely made of impersonal spirit or ground of being and only *appears* "material."

2. **A personal being created the universe using no preexisting material—creation *ex nihilo*.** This has always been the position of the three monotheistic or Abrahamic religions: Judaism, Christianity, and Islam. It is the basic assumption of the Hebrew Bible and it is stated clearly in Genesis 1, "In the beginning God created the heavens and the earth." A generation ago the idea of the Creator as a personal being would require little explanation. Today, with the unstated assumptions of Pantheism being blended with traditional conceptions of God; this may require some defining. A personal being is one with the attributes of personhood, such as knowing things, being capable of emotion, having a will, etc. To be God, such a being would have to be "The greatest Being that can be conceived of." (St. Anselm, ca. 1100). This means it would have the omni properties— all knowing (omniscient), all powerful (omnipotent), and

all good (omnibenevolent). I go to the trouble of stating what should be obvious but as we saw in the chapter on worldview thinking, what is obvious in one philosophical system is not obvious in another. In the chapter on the cosmological argument, I'll make the case for a personal creator as a necessary being. To put it more simply, I find the idea of an impersonal being incoherent and a result of the culture absorbing Eastern thinking and the attendant abandonment of logic for semantic mysticism (i.e., word games that make things sound spiritual).

3. **The universe came out of nothing.** This idea has become popular with the advent of quantum mechanics (QM). It is an effect without a cause, which is linguistic nonsense. It is based on the idea that virtual particles pop out of the vacuum energy of a quantum field. But a quantum field (contra Stephen Hawking) is not "nothing"; it is still *something*. This option is therefore merely a variation on number one, with the quantum field being what is eternal and self-existent.

4. **The universe caused itself.** This means that the universe would have to have existed before it existed. In other words, it would have to be and not be at the same time in the same sense. This is a logical contradiction but is having a resurgence under QM. This is a self-defeating version of number one.

I will dismiss option numbers three and four as popular notions based upon scientific and philosophical error. The weirdness of

40

QM is fertile ground for generating nonsense. People bound by logic consider numbers one and two as live options. Remember that since facts are interpreted through the lens of one's worldview, our worldviews strongly affect how we develop and assess evidence. This is why we must decide among Naturalism, Pantheism, and Theism before we examine the case for Jesus' resurrection. The evidence cannot be held hostage to a worldview out of which it did not come.

In the next chapter I'll show that the universe had a beginning, eliminating number one, and that the cause of the beginning, by its nature, must have the attributes of the God described in number two. In subsequent chapters I'll present further arguments pointing to a personal God.

If a beginning to the universe is accepted, the decision then has to be between Deism: a transcendent creator God who is not presently involved with the Creation in any effective way. And classical Theism: an infinite, yet personal God who is involved with his creation.

If classical Theism is allowed, then the Creator could be expected to reveal himself in some way. This revelation could be found by looking at design in nature, some sacred scripture, or perhaps even by the Creator making a personal appearance. On the individual level, revelation could also come through a personal encounter, though such encounters may have limited evidential value for others.

I believe that all these types of revelation support Christianity. The case for Christian Theism is a cumulative case. The arguments

I will present can stand alone as probable, but are also mutually reinforcing. As a cumulative case they should lead to an effective certitude when appreciated in their fullness.

In preparing for the next chapters, note that most skeptics like to take each argument, one at a time, and find something to doubt about each. This is certainly possible as none of these arguments is indubitable. Note, however, that these skeptics are notorious for applying severe scrutiny to other worldviews while avoiding scrutiny of their own. This is either blindness or intellectual dishonesty. So the skeptic's tactic is to divide and conquer, hoping to show that the Christian case is a series of leaky buckets from which the water will eventually drain out.

But the Christian case is more like a collection of leaky buckets (Only in the sense that *some* may personalyg doubt certain claims.) nested together in such a way that the holes do not line up, since they address different issues, therefore the whole collection will hold water. The skeptic claims that a chain is only as strong as its weakest link, but a more appropriate analogy is chain mail armor, composed of intricately interconnected links—you can pop one link, but the suit of armor will still hold together.

The case for the historical resurrection is robust and could stand on its own for the willing believer, as it did for me. I found the evidence for the resurrection to be so good as to lead me to belief in a personal creator God, but for many people it seems to work the other way around. If a Theistic worldview were not presupposed, it would not matter how good the evidence is for the resurrection. If you presuppose Naturalism or Pantheism to be true, you will just have no place to hang the evidence for Christian Theism where it makes any sense. Jesus' resurrection will be dismissed as either a myth or projection of emotional need (Naturalism) or a natural outworking of the realization of Jesus' own godhood (Pantheism).

Instead of relying on presupposed worldviews and forcing the evidence to fit our faiths, hopefully we can open our minds and see which worldview genuinely fits the facts. I am sympathetic to the difficulty of being open-minded. I am loathe to give up Christian Theism because it gives me what I want—personal significance and immortality. I know some of you are more invested in something else, like personal autonomy.

But neither of us can escape what is ultimately real. And neither of us can escape the fact that there is at least some evidence for the other guy's worldview. So let's look at the evidence!

PART II

THE EVIDENCE THAT
DEMANDS A VERDICT:
THE BOOK OF NATURE

THE COSMOLOGICAL
ARGUMENT

• • •

This is perhaps the most difficult subject I will present. It is actually kind of fun when the light goes on. I hope I have made it accessible. I certainly had to play around with it for a while before it became intuitive for me. It provides a background demonstrating that a deity with the characteristics of the God of the Bible is at least plausible, if not more plausible than its denial.

In one form or another, the cosmological argument has been around since ancient times—at least since Aristotle. In postulating how the universe came into existence, Aristotle argued that there must be a First Unmoved Mover, which is God.[17] The Hebrews, by revelation, understood God to be a living, sentient, non-embodied eternal being who is the source of order in the cosmos. Though the word *cosmos* is often used synonymously with *universe, cosmos* actually means order (as opposed to chaos).

While observing the diverse peoples and cultures around him during the first century AD, St. Paul says in Romans 1:18 that all men know God because He has been revealed in nature. Psalm 19:1-2 says, "The heavens tell of the glory of God; the skies display his marvelous craftsmanship. Day after day they continue to speak;

---

17   W. T. Jones, *History of Western Philosophy 2nd edition, vol. I* (New York: Harcourt, Brace and World, 1969), 230-232.

and night after night they make him known." The Psalmist is saying that the created order tells us something about God. Paul goes on to say in his letter to the Romans, that men suppress this innate knowledge because they want to live contrary to what the divine mind has written on their consciences.

So from the earliest times, man, even when wholly removed from Biblical revelation, concluded from observing the universe that a divine mind must exist.

Over the centuries this basic idea has been developed in various ways. In Christian thinking, it is most associated with Thomas Aquinas, who lived in the thirteenth century. But modern (post-Kantian) philosophy has done a good job of beating up traditional cosmological arguments for the existence of God.

However, at least one form of the argument still carries substantial weight: It is known as the Kalam cosmological argument. An Islamic scholar, al-Ghazali, who lived at about the time of Aquinas, developed it, and its leading proponent today is William Lane Craig, Ph.D. It has been tested and critiqued in leading philosophical journals, as well as through debates at many universities. The Kalam argument appears robust simply because so much continues to be written against it.

Of course, for every argument there is a counterargument, and a counter to that. I have looked at several of the layers of the argumentation on this, only some of which I reproduce here. For those interested in studying the matter further, I suggest Dr. Craig's book *Reasonable Faith*.[18]

---

18 W. L. Craig, *Reasonable Faith*, 3rd ed. (Wheaton, IL, Crossway, 2008), 111.

The Kalam cosmological argument may be formulated as follows:

1. Whatever begins to exist has a cause.

2. The universe began to exist.

3. Conclusion: The universe has a cause.

The Kalam argument has a logically sound structure, so if premises one and two are both true, then the conclusion must follow. So any problem with the argument must be in premise one or two. So let's see if they appear reasonable.

Dr. Craig says that one seems obviously true, at least more so than its negation. It is rooted in the intuition that something cannot come into existence from complete nothingness. To suggest that things could just pop out of nothing is to forgo serious thinking and resort to magic. Premise one is also constantly confirmed by experience.

Atheists, who generally maintain a high view of science, have the strongest motivations to accept that one is true. After all, scientific investigation involves analyzing strings of causes and effects. For every event (effect), a cause must be identified. In fact the causal closer (i.e., the universe is a closed system of cause and effect with no outside influence to affect it) of the universe is part of the very definition of Naturalism. Dr. Craig is surprised that many Atheists who reject God as a first cause to the universe still affirm the validity of one.

So how do skeptics try to avoid the divine implications of premise one?

Some argue that if one must be applied to the universe, then it must also be applied to God. Thus, God must have a beginning and there must be a preexisting cause of God. But note that one states that "whatever begins" has a cause. By definition, God is eternal and timeless (this will be explained further) and therefore does not have a cause. But is the Theist using semantics to attempt to escape this trap? Is God's "timelessness" really intelligible?

The Kalam argument holds that time is finite. According to the German mathematician David Hilbert, time is finite because it is impossible to have infinity of real objects or events. For the physical universe (including time and space) to have existed forever (and therefore have no beginning), it would have to exist as an infinite chain of cause and effect. This would entail a real infinity of objects and moments, which is a mathematical impossibility. According to mathematics, only potential infinities "exist"—in other words, infinity is a limiting idea, not a physical thing. So an infinite self-existent universe, in time or space, is impossible.

This inescapably implies that two is true—that the universe had a beginning. However, we are still looking at whether God can escape the trap of the first Kalam premise. This can be put simply as the question of a six year old: "Daddy, who made God?"

By existing in a timeless and immaterial state, God is not constrained by time or a finite cause-and-effect chain. Causality in the material sense requires time; it cannot occur in the absence of time. Additionally, being immaterial, God lacks extension (the property of a body that occupies space), thus eliminating the physical space requirement too. As a result, God is not trapped by one—the need for a cause—whereas the universe, containing space and time, undoubtedly is.

Another objection is that if causation happens only in time, how did God cause the universe before creating time? Dr. Craig has argued persuasively that God can support a space/time universe as simultaneity, i.e. as a pillow supports a bowling ball. There need be no "in time" for this action. God's support of the universe is non-temporal.

Another way to conceive of the Kalam argument is to suppose you are now standing in the present, where $t = P$ (time equals present). If the universe goes back to eternity past, then it "began" in the infinite past. With time ticking forward at a finite rate, it is not possible to ever get from $t = -\infty$ (infinite past) to $t = P$. This should be as obvious as the fact that you can't get from $t = p$ to the infinite future. That would be the same as counting to infinity. You can always add one more number. I know you can't do it because I tried it once. I gave up after about three hours! You cannot count forward from past infinity to *now* any more than you can count from now to future infinity. You cannot cross an infinity of time any more than you can cross an infinite distance. Infinite time and infinite space cannot be real entities. An infinite self-existent universe does not hold up to philosophical or mathematical scrutiny. The universe (and time itself) had a beginning. Anything with a beginning has a cause. The universe has a cause: a timeless, immaterial being (pure existence), which conforms to a traditional description of God. The premises of the Kalam cosmological argument appear true, so this conclusion must follow.

While the mathematical and philosophical arguments backing the Kalam argument can be difficult to follow, and might seem like verbal sleight of hand, there are several scientific arguments as well.

The theory of general relativity, as expanded by Rodger Penrose and Stephen Hawking, states that all matter, energy, space, and time had a coincident beginning. But many scientists are critical of the notion of a beginning, arguing that general relativity breaks down at Planck time, or $1/10^{43}$ seconds after t = 0. To quote astronomer Arthur Eddington:

> Philosophically, the notion of a beginning of the present order of Nature is repugnant to me...I see no way around it; but whether future developments of science will find an escape I cannot predict.[19]

Critics hope that this tiny fragment of ignorance of the first infinitesimal fraction of the first second after the instant of the big bang will save them from the dreaded singularity, the alleged state of the universe at the creation moment, where all the laws of physics broke down, and from the corresponding conclusion that the universe had a beginning.

For many years now, *Scientific American* and a host of other science publications, professional and popular, have been arguing for alternative cosmologies in the hopes of getting around the beginning of the universe, which seems to entail God as a first cause.

The first two space-time "cones", shown in Figure 2, illustrate Big Bang models with an absolute beginning. The third cone illustrates a "rounded off" space-time or, more accurately put, a

---

19 A. Eddington, "The End of the World: From the Standpoint of Mathematical Physics," *Nature,* 127 (1931), 450. The astute reader will note that this is a decidedly unscientific statement coming from a working scientist. Though I don't know exactly why Dr. Eddington finds this idea repugnant, but it's quite likely because this bit of scientifically and mathematically determined data doesn't fit within his naturalistic worldview.

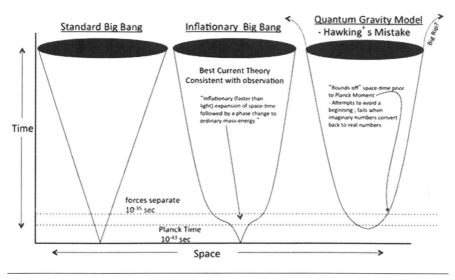

FIGURE 2. Three Models of Cosmic History.

conversion of time into space as an attempt to avoid a beginning in time. This model was originally proposed by Steven Hawking, but fails when the equations are converted from imaginary numbers back to real numbers.

The oscillating or "bang-crunch" model, shown in Figure 3, was popular with religions favoring reincarnation because of the

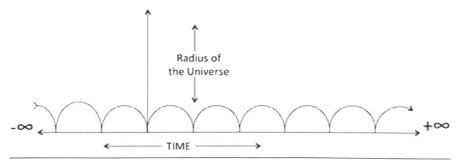

FIGURE 3. The Oscillating Universe Model.

infinite repetitions. In addition to the Second Law or heat death problem, the way the cycles are laid out on a number line illustrates the impossibility of getting to "now" from the infinite past—the heart of the Kalam Cosmological Argument. It would also require even more extreme fine tuning than the inflationary big bang just to get it through a few cycles.

Another model that attempts to avoid a beginning is the vacuum fluctuation model, shown in Figure 4. This model has been

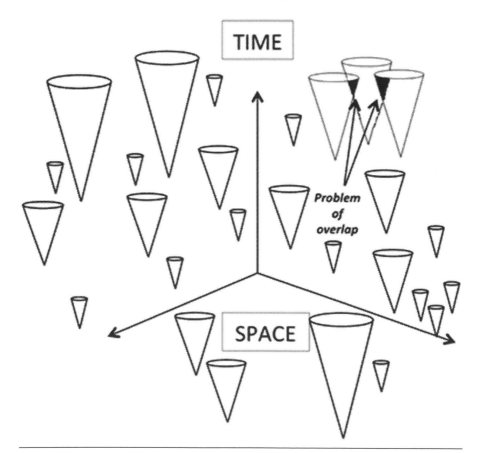

FIGURE 4. The Vacuum Fluctuation Model.

recently argued as a way to get universes out of nothing. Proposed by Lawrence Krauss, it involves a past-eternal space-time "foam" that has fluctuations that spawn new universes. But the "nothing" is really something and the infinite/eternal space time "foam" would eventually spawn a universe at all points and we would be at infinite density—not exactly a life friendly situation.

All of this should have come to an end in 2003. Guth and Vilenkin's formulation of the space/time theorem establishes that any universe, which has had, on average, a state of cosmic expansion, cannot be eternal in the past and must have a space-time boundary or beginning. This conclusion does not stand upon a particular physical description of the universe prior to Planck time. This theory puts an end to all models that try to escape a beginning, especially the current naturalistic favorite, which is the eternal inflationary multiverse, namely an infinite set of time/space universes that stretches back to infinity. This infinite branching and budding model falls prey to the Kalam argument exactly as a single infinite universe. One reason for hanging on to this model, as we will see in the next chapter on design, is that the multiverse appears to be the best hope for defeating the argument that the universe is designed and fine-tuned specifically for our existence—the anthropic principle.

The next scientific argument is quite simple. The second law of thermodynamics states that all systems will eventually reach a state of thermal equilibrium—meaning the exact same temperature everywhere, over infinite time. However, our universe clearly consists of hot and cold regions (such as stars and empty space).

This means that the universe has not been here forever. If the past were infinite we would see no temperature differences anywhere. This "heat death" appears to be the inevitable future of our universe, unless the universe is acted on from outside itself.

All cosmic models—including oscillating (reincarnating), branching, budding, and colliding five-dimensional membranes—all wind down according to the second law, meaning that at one time they were all wound up at the beginning. The second law has never been questioned, except by those trying to get the patent office to consider their perpetual motion machine![20]

So Theists have a number of strong arguments supporting the idea that the universe had a beginning and that its Creator is separate from the universe. The idea of a created universe must, at a minimum, be considered more plausible that its denial, giving justification to Theism.

The next question is this: is the Creator personal or impersonal?

Thinking about the implications of the above, it is apparent that the first cause, having created space and time, must transcend space and time. Lacking time, it must be changeless and eternal, at least with respect to us. It must be very powerful, considering it created the universe without any preexisting material. One could say it is infinitely powerful, since the distance between being and non-being is infinite, whether it is for an electron or a universe. Dr. Craig states that such a transcendent cause can plausibly be taken to be personal.

---

20 An excellent description of alternative universes can be read in Chapters 3 and 4 of William Lane Craig's *Reasonable Faith*.

How so? Oxford philosopher Richard Swinburne points out that there are two types of causal explanations: (a) scientific explanations, in terms of laws and initial conditions which are repeatable, and (b) personal explanations, in terms of agents and their volitions which may be unique occurrences. It appears self evident that free agents (freethinking persons) can cause changes in the material world. You can prove it to yourself right now by simply raising your hand and saying, "I just raised my hand." If you did this, then you have just experienced a properly basic (needs no defense) intuition that "you" (a person) chose to raise your hand and thus affect the material world of your own volition.[21]

Now I realize that a committed Naturalist will point to a material chain of cause and effect to explain his/her actions something like this: "Our universe was spawned by a big bang stemming from infinite alternate universes; the matter and energy coalesced into stars and planets; on Earth, material life randomly evolved over billions of years; human beings eventually came into existence; I am one of those human beings; in the random course of events I read this essay and was "caused" by this chain to raise my hand in response to the words typed on the page." But if all that materialistic dogma is true, then we may as well abandon the pursuit of truth, since humans are not really freethinking agents. Under Naturalism, we are deterministically programmed machines, and all philosophical discussions are devoid of intellectual and moral merit. If we are nothing more than complex rocks, debates are pointless.

---

21   R. Swinburne, *Is There a God?* (USA, Oxford University Press, 1997), 4.

This brings us back to the universe's first cause.

Dr. Craig writes:

Now the first state of the universe *cannot* have a scientific explanation, since there is nothing before it, and therefore it cannot be accounted for in terms of laws operating on initial conditions. It can only be accounted for in terms of an agent and his volitions, a personal explanation.[22]

Agent causation requires intent and action. These are what make the agent "personal."

The fact that the agent is an immaterial mind means it has no problem with the infinities associated with space and time. It does not need a cause, unlike the universe.

To conclude, we've made a positive case that the first cause of the universe is immaterial, unlimited in power, and personal. This looks a lot like the God described in the Bible.

Besides giving support for classical Theism, the cosmological argument has negative implications for other philosophies and religions. We have already shown the devastating implications for Naturalism, but the same holds true for Eastern Pantheism. Pantheism, like Naturalism, says that the universe is all there is (per Carl Sagan in *Cosmos*). In Pantheism, the difference is that the universe is reduced to an appearance and is not really "real." In one sense the denial of the universe as merely an appearance (to avoid the real problems of space and time) is fallacious. The real world, as objective and distinct from us, is undeniable, since to deny the appearance of the real world is to use an appearance to deny an appearance, and that is self-refuting.

---

22   W. L. Craig, *Reasonable Faith*, 3rd ed. (Wheaton, Crossway, 2008), 152-153.

Worldview philosopher Dr. Max Sotak says, "I don't see how a Pantheist could piggyback on an argument of any kind, since there is no rational or discursive mind to employ an argument. Personalism again gets in the way, since impersonal minds—at least given our experience of mind—don't think."[23]

Those who know more of the details of Eastern philosophy may say I have failed to distinguish between Monism (no differences, only Brahman) and the Pantheism of Ramanuja, which holds that differences exist but are part of Brahman. In either case, the beginning of the universe is a problem. Dr. Paul Copan, co-author of *Creation Out Of Nothing*, says for the Pantheist there is no personal agent that could bring about a universe or dramatically alter the metaphysical landscape (e.g., bring about a material universe out of nothing). Contra Pantheism, a personal agent would be necessary to bring about this new state of affairs. For the monist there is no material that would begin to exist. It is an illusion or an appearance, which we've dealt with.[24]

Pantheistic ideas may still be taken on faith or mystical intuition, but seem to lack the robust justification of Theism. They may still have utility as personal philosophies or ethical systems, but any claims of correspondence to reality or moral force are forfeited.

The Kalam cosmological argument effectively eliminates both Naturalism and Pantheism as viable worldviews, leaving the Middle Eastern monotheistic religions as the only ones with a claim on reality as normally conceived.

---

23 Max Sotak (2010) personal communication.

24 P. Copan (2010) personal communication.

THE ARGUMENT FROM DESIGN

● ● ●

I n case the material in the last chapter seemed obscure or a slight-of-hand, I believe you'll find this material to be both more intuitive and grounded in observational science. The recent conversion of leading Atheist philosopher, Antony Flew, to some sort of minimal Theism was based on the design argument. This caused something of a firestorm. The *New York Times* wrote that, in his dotage, Flew had fallen victim to the kindly ministrations of his Christian dialogue partners. The fact that Flew rejects most Christian doctrines shows that this attempt to discredit him is baseless. Flew says the arguments from teleology (purpose) are impressive and could not have been imagined fifty years ago.[25]

The apparent design in nature has traditionally been viewed as a strong argument for the existence of a conscious mind. This intuitive idea reached its apex with William Paley, circa 1700s, and his watchmaker argument. Paley said that if you walk across a field and find a ticking watch, you make the inference this is not an

---

25 A. Flew, *There is A God* (San Francisco, HarperOne, 2008) 95. Dr. Flew died in April, 2010 at the age of 87. He was so close to belief, I hope he made it over the line. He had all the information at his disposal. Flew was the son of a Methodist preacher and was favorably disposed to the Bible as literature, contra the Koran, and was an admirer of the writings of St. Paul. Unlike the current crop of Atheists, he tried to use good arguments and charity towards all. I hope to meet him someday.

artifact of nature. However, with the advent of Darwin's theory of evolution, the simplistic form of the watchmaker argument was discredited among the majority of scientists. Philosophers point out that it's an argument by analogy, which is only as good as the similarity of the things being compared; scientists are quick to point out the differences between living and non-living systems. But these differences are contrary to Materialism's grand narrative that life and non-life are essentially the same. One merely ascends a scale of complexity from molecules to man with continuity at each step.

But this does not mean that the design issue has been settled. Paley's watchmaker argument is back and this time it's on steroids! Microbiology has discovered a large number of systems that are not just analogous to machines but *are* machines in the strict sense of the word. The analogy to a found artifact, like a watch, holds at the cellular level, thus the need for a watchmaker. At this point the Naturalist backs up a step and asks why a watch couldn't make itself, given enough time of course. The problem is each of the systems and subsystems in the cell are *irreducibly complex*. Such systems lack function until *all* the parts show up at the same time and have a waiting instruction set (code) to put them together in the right order. This is a fantastic requirement to any fair-minded scientist. The problem of irreducible complexity caused microbiologist Michel Behe to break ranks with the Darwinian "small steps" approach for which the scientific establishment has never forgiven (or refuted) him.[26]

---

26   M. Behe, *Darwin's Black Box*, (New York, Free Press, 2006), 39.

The intelligent design community has made powerful arguments, from both microbiology and information theory. The attempt to discredit them as "religiously motivated" commits the genetic fallacy—that the truth of an idea is dependent on where it came from. These arguments claim that the Darwinian mechanism of natural selection—acting on small random variations in genetic structures—is incapable of producing the full range of life forms that we see in our world. In other words, random chance together with natural selection cannot account for the massive amounts of new information that must be added to simpler life forms to make more complex forms. This debate is so emotional and politically loaded that I will sidestep it for the moment. Instead, we will work with the "simple" sciences of astronomy and physics, which lack the mythical power of natural selection acting on random mutations.

We can all agree that the universe is massive. But it is a startling fact that if the initial mass of the universe were different by an amount equal to the mass of a single dime, or 1 part in 10^{60}, the universe would either have re-collapsed on itself after its initial expansion (one dime more mass) or expanded into diffuse gas that is incapable of galaxy formation (one dime less). The fine-tuning of the energy density (so-called dark energy, an expansion factor) is precise to $1/10^{120}$. The initial rate of the universe's expansion rate must be set 1 part in 10^{55}.[27] Most astoundingly, according to Oxford mathematician Roger Penrose, one esoteric parameter, the "original phase-space volume," must be fine tuned to an astounding

---

27 http://www.godandscience.org/apologetics/designun.html

1/10 to the 10th to the 123rd power ($1/10^{10^{123}}$).[28] [Note: I had to stack the exponents this way because there isn't enough room in the universe to write all the zeros!]

Just these three initial conditions are so improbable that no knowledgeable scientist appeals to random chance for an explanation. Yet the atheistic hope of some underlying non-divine "necessity" for these conditions to exist continues to burn, and non-testable cosmic models can be found regularly in publications like *Scientific American*.

The physical laws of the universe, such as general relativity, electromagnetism, etc., came into being at the beginning of the universe. Each of these laws has a numerical constant associated with it. The speed of light, the gravitational constant, Planck's constant, and several others must all be held to very precise limits in order for life of any form to exist. It is implausible to think of any "necessity" that these constants should be what they are.

Another fine-tuning example involves electrons and protons. The electron and the proton have opposite but equal electric charges, so it would seem natural to assume that they have the same mass. However, a proton's mass is 1,800 times the electron's mass. This ratio is necessary for chemistry to work in such a way as to support biological life. Why is this ratio the life supporting number and not something else?

Planetary constraints are also severe. Reports of extra-solar and perhaps earthlike planets do injustice to the difficulties of forming a

---

28   Lee Strobel, *The Case For a Creator: A Journalist Investigates Scientific Evidence That Points Toward God* (2005, Zondervan, Grand Rapids), 135.

life-sustaining planet. The sun not only needs to have just the right gravitational pull (mass) and luminosity, but also the correct mixture of metals. It is not just a matter of adjusting the planets distance from its sun to allow for liquid water, as popular science would lead you to believe. In any solar system that deviates just slightly from sun/earth parameters, various orbital instabilities crop up that preclude advanced life. Nearby supernova (massive exploding stars) must have been near to our proto solar system to provide the necessary heavy metals needed for organic life. The amount of radioactive minerals in the planet must be adequate to heat the core to produce a magnetic field as a shield from cosmic radiation. The heat from these minerals would also drive plate tectonics, which is necessary to recycle the minerals that are required for life.

Former Cal Tech astronomer Dr. Hugh Ross lists these design constraints on his website (www.reasons.org). Over the years the list has grown from a few dozen to several hundred. Multiplication of these improbabilities shows that the existence of an earthlike planet anywhere in the universe is very, *very* unlikely to occur in a universe formed only through natural, unguided processes. But of course, an intelligent all-powerful Creator can create as many habitable planets as it chooses.

The origin of life is something that the popular press would lead you to believe is almost solved. But scientific researchers in the field have stated that all former naturalistic hypotheses (warm little ponds of primordial soup, the RNA world, genetic organization on crystals, etc.) are abject failures, and as of now not a single fruitful line of research exists.

To support a naturalistic explanation of the universe, not only must difficult physical and chemical problems be overcome, but the origin of biological information (genetic codes) must also be explained. Matter and energy are the stuff of science, but information is not. Because of this, there is no reason to expect that science will ever offer an explanation for the origin of biological information. The instruction set of even the simplest genome is similar in size and complexity to an encyclopedia and for the first life form to randomly come into being would be like writing an encyclopedia by dumping Scrabble letters out the window. And by definition, *first life* must have happened without a Darwinian mechanism to direct the process. "Survival of the fittest" first assumes the arrival of the fit enough.

Finally, the Darwinian mechanism itself is not as robust as it appears to be. In just taking a cursory look at the life forms on our world, there seems to be intuitive support for evolution—life seems interconnected in some sense, morphologically, genetically, and chemically. Life forms do change over time. I have no problem with the continuity of life or common ancestry, although they are by no means certain. The gaps in the fossil record may well be real. The real question is what mechanism moves evolution onward and upward? These terms have no meaning in nature. They imply direction and goals and therefore make no sense in an unguided world.

Natural selection seems to be a force for stasis, not for constant biological change over millions of years. As noted above, it is by no means clear that the mechanism of random mutation, acted upon by natural selection, is adequate to produce the complexity of life we see on planet earth. It is the mutations and not the natural selection part of Darwinism that must drive the process towards something new. Molecular biologist Douglas Axe performed mutational sensitivity tests on enzymes to measure the likelihood that a string of amino acids would generate a functional protein. The article, published in the *Journal of Molecular Biology*, showed that functional protein folds might occur as rarely as once in 10^{77} amino acid sequences. Since there are not nearly that many amino acid sequences in the entire universe, this is the same as saying that it is impossible. This would be like shooting an arrow into the Milky Way galaxy and hitting one pre-selected atom.[29]

Some of my readers trained in biology may take exception at this point, noting that they see changes in genotype corresponding to changes in phenotype. This involves things like LINEs, SINEs, gene duplication, chromosomal splicing, etc. I don't understand most of this, but I do know that it amounts to a rearrangement of *existing* genetic code—changes to what is already there. But this only accounts for variation among the lower taxa. To move much past the genera/family level requires writing new code. This, according to microbiologist Michel Behe is to move past "the edge of evolution" and into the improbabilities in the previous paragraph, into the necessity of design.[30]

---

29   Douglas A. Axe, "Extreme Functional Sensitivity to Conservative Amino Acid Changes on Enzyme Exteriors," *Journal of Molecular Biology*, Vol. 301 (2000): 585-595.

30   M. Behe, *Edge of Evolution*. (New York, Free Press, 2008) 166.

Naturalistic scientists, especially in private, concede many of these arguments. There is more than some scientific dissatisfaction with Darwinism, and alternative naturalistic explanations are being sought, such as punctuated equilibrium (PUNC-ECK) and evolutionary developmental (EVO-DEVO) biology. The former lacks a plausible mechanism while the latter is just pushing design to an earlier location. Ironically, this idea of "front loading" design into the earliest life, to "turn on" under the right environmental conditions looks even more like intelligent causation. Of course philosophical Naturalists, as well as Theists committed to the methods of natural science in their work, *must* come up with naturalistic explanations because supernatural ones are not permitted under the rules of the scientific magisterium.

Some theistic evolutionists believe that the front-loading of biological information is built into the laws of physics at the beginning and thus hope to save both God and Darwin. But there is just no plausible connection between chemistry and physics and the problem of biological information. If front loading is the answer, it's not in laws of science, it's in philosophy and theology and that's back to design.

But if the evidence for intelligent design is becoming increasingly clear, why is it not more publicly acknowledged? In a *New York Times* article Harvard geneticist Richard Lewontin, developer of population genetics, candidly stated that we must adhere to naturalistic explanations regardless of how flimsy they are because we cannot afford to "let a divine foot in the door." After his lecture about these problems, I asked a prominent origin of life researcher from New York University, "Why not appeal to intelligent design?" He told me bluntly, "Well, that wouldn't be doing science."

As Phillip Johnson points out in his book, *Darwin on Trial*, materialistic scientists have cleverly redefined the word *science* to be synonymous with Naturalism. That way, they can conveniently label naturalistic explanations for the universe as scientific and dismiss agent caused explanations for the universe as unscientific. So instead of following the evidence wherever it may lead, science has intentionally limited itself to the pursuit of material causes for the universe, no matter how inadequate the explanations.[31] This works fine as long as their foundational assumptions are correct, but will lead nowhere if their assumptions are incorrect.[32]

By *philosophically* assuming that there must be a Materialist ("scientific") explanation for everything we observe in the universe, including the existence, complexity, and diversity of life, these scientists have closed their minds to the implications of the scientific data. Unfortunately for their "religion," the evidence increasingly points to intelligent, non-random causes.

It should be noted that intelligent design is not an appeal from ignorance or a "God of the gaps" argument. It is true that many things once attributed to "the gods" have been explained by modern science. However, things are now moving in the opposite direction.

---

31 P. Johnson, *Darwin on Trial,* (Downers Grove, InterVarsity Press, 2010) 146-147.

32 We cannot overstate this point. The universe was caused. If by material forces, then materialistic science has a chance of figuring out the answers. If by an intelligent Creator, material science will *never* find the cause because it has ruled out this possibility *a priori*. This is not science, but philosophy. The materialistic worldview has no place to put non-material causes. Once again, the philosophical commitment determines what can and cannot be discovered.

What was once explained by random chance (initial conditions, origin of life, etc.) is now conceded as statistically impossible. The gaps are now *growing* instead of shrinking. This has left the Naturalists with their own "chance of the gaps" problem, where they are increasingly forced to find implausibly complex natural causes to fill the growing gaps in their explanations.

Naturalists hope to bypass the enormous statistical improbability that this universe, apparently fine-tuned for carbon-based life, could have come into existence by chance. They put their hope in the idea of an infinite multiverse, as we saw in the last chapter. The multiverse idea is that our universe is not the only universe—an infinite ensemble of material universes exists through infinite time. Given infinite universes and infinite time, even the most statistically improbable events (such as the aforementioned fine-tuning of this particular universe) will eventually occur an infinite number of times!

For one thing, the eternal infinite multiverse will still fall prey to the problem of David Hilbert's mathematics—the impossibility of an infinite set of real objects (in this case universes) to exist.

One attempt to ground the multiverse in something more than speculation is the appeal to string theory. This attempt to multiply the probabilistic resources of Materialism still seems to fall short of what is necessary to overcome the multiplication of all the design parameters. The equations of string theory are said to yield 10^{500} universes. This is a lot, but far short of infinity, and far short of the number needed to produce even one universe with the fine-tuning we see. Besides, string theory remains a theoretical hypothesis, and no one knows whether it's true. It's also unclear how to solve those equations and whether the solutions would yield any life supporting universes. These difficulties are often glossed over in popular science media. They are not just speculation, but according to one physicist, they are "speculation squared."[33]

Within the framework of the infinite multiverse, everything "natural" must happen. Perhaps worm holes (placed on either side of the Red Sea) allowed gravitational fields from alternate universes to part the waters just in time for the Hebrews to march through the sea with Moses in the lead (the worm holes randomly closed to let the waters crush the Egyptian army). Even Darwinism falls prey to this universal acid. How does the Darwinist know he is not a brain in a vat being fed his ideas by a mad scientist? This scenario *must* happen in some possible world. Clearly the multiverse can be used to prove *anything*, and therefore proves nothing.

Because the concept of science is built on freethinking intelligence—which a purely naturalistic universe cannot produce—science itself implicitly assumes intelligent design. Evolution might produce something with some competence at thinking but not someone with true comprehension

To bring William Paley's watchmaker argument full circle, archeologists clearly accept the idea of design—after all, they

---

33 H. Ross, "Astronomical Evidences for a Personal, Transcendent God," *The Creation Hypothesis*, ed. J. P. Moreland (Downers Grove, IL, InterVarsity Press, 1994) 156. Of course there's nothing wrong with speculative thinking in science. That's where new theories come from. What's objectionable is when wildly speculative and unproven ideas are sold to the non-science public as having more weight than they actually do, especially when these ideas are sold in order to prop up a theory that's in trouble.

routinely distinguish man-made artifacts from the actions of erosion. The search for extraterrestrials is predicated on the idea that we can distinguish an intelligent signal from a naturally occurring one. For example, some years ago, a regular beep-beep signal was detected by a radio telescope. A design inference was made. This turned out to be false; the beep-beep was generated by two rapidly orbiting neutron stars (a pulsar). The lesson here is that regularity—order—is *not* a hallmark of design. Design is characterized by complex, specified information, such as what is found in books or computer programs. This specified complexity is exactly what we find in DNA. Natural processes can only form regular patterns (by law) or random noise (by chance). If you are interested in further reading on this subject, Dr. William Dembski has formulated this distinction into a rigorous mathematical "design filter" in his groundbreaking work, *Intelligent Design*.[34]

The argument from design is not a religious argument, although it has religious implications. While the cosmological argument points to an infinite personal Creator that is separate from the universe (a.k.a. Theism), the design argument carries no such specificity. However it seems that whatever designed the physics of the universe would logically be *outside* the universe. Design certainly points to a super intellect present in, or more likely outside this universe (the cosmological argument). The God of the Bible and the Creation story in Genesis, properly interpreted, are fully compatible with what scientists know about design.

---

34 W. Dembski, *Intelligent Design* (Downers Grove, IL, InterVarsity Press, 1999).

PART III

══

JESUS AND THE BIBLE: HISTORY OR MYTH?

"Jesus Studies" Since the Enlightenment

S tudies into the life of Jesus inevitably involve the question of miracles. Those scholars who are at least *open* to the miraculous can objectively examine the gospel accounts of Jesus' life. Those who already reject the possibility of miracles end up trying to rewrite Jesus' story to fit within their own philosophical paradigms. Chapter 4 on worldviews demonstrated how "evidence," like that for miracles, is filtered through one's set of control assumptions about how the world works.

Prior to the Enlightenment in the seventeenth century, the miracles of Jesus, and especially his resurrection, were considered sufficient to prove his claim as the son of God. But with the advent of the age of reason, the church and Biblical authority came under attack. While notables such as Sir Isaac Newton remained committed Christians, their work seemed to weaken the claims of the supernatural. Appearing to operate by immutable laws, Newton's clockwork universe was regarded as a closed system of cause and effect. Most intellectuals still held that God was required as a first cause but that after "winding up" the universe, God walked away and left it to run on its own (Deism). In the subsequent centuries, science was used to explain more and more, and the notion of a God was required to explain less and less. This became known as the "God of the gaps" problem—the more holes science filled in, the less need there was for God.

In the last chapter I showed that modern science is actually enlarging the gaps and is coming to the realization that there *is* the need for a transcendent explanation. The gap problem cuts both ways. Here is where you begin to see another gap, between science and philosophy—the clash in worldviews. If God does not intervene in the physical universe, he also need not intervene in history, perform miracles, answer prayer, or leave any written revelation.

In philosophy there was a similar situation. René Descartes, known for his famous catchphrase "I think, therefore I am," was working on a proof of the existence of God. He was looking for a foundational starting point, something that could not be doubted. Unfortunately, Descartes' argument for the existence of God is not particularly compelling, but his approach had a profound impact. By making man, or more specifically man's *thinking*, the starting point for all things, he effectively cut man off from anything outside himself, like God. Contrary to his intention, he expanded the role of humanism, which was already on the rise from the Renaissance. Millennia earlier in Greece, Protagoras claimed, "Man is the measure of all things."—a reminder that ideas in philosophy tend to come back under other names. Humanism is not a new phenomenon.

Most modern thinkers who reject miracles trace their reasoning to the Scottish skeptic David Hume (1711–1776). Hume provided what many view as the most formidable of all challenges to a supernatural perspective: the notion that miracles are "incredible." He didn't mean impossible—he was enough of a skeptic to avoid saying anything with certainty. He simply meant that miracles are not credible. Although there have been ample criticisms of Hume's rationale, naturalistic philosophers tend to ignore these criticisms completely. Hume boasts:

> I flatter myself, that I have discovered an argument of a like nature... which...will, with the wise and learned, be an everlasting check to all kinds of superstitious delusion, and...will be useful as long as the world endures.[35]

His reasoning goes like this: (1) "A miracle is a violation of the laws of nature," (2) "experience has established these laws," (3) "this same experience is uniformly against every miracle." Therefore, (4) this constitutes proof "...against the existence of any miracle."[36]

Notice that Hume stated, "A miracle is a violation of the laws of nature" and in his words "...unalterable experience has established these laws..." However, Hume's "unalterable experience" is question begging—it assumes that miracles do not exist. If you presume to know that all experience is uniform in advance of the evidence, how can you possibly know that all human experience will confirm or deny the existence of miracles without access to all possible experiences, past, present, and future?[37]

---

35 D. Hume, *An Enquiry Concerning Human Understanding*, ed. Eric Steinberg (Indianapolis, Hackett, 1993) 73.

36 Ibid., 76-77.

37 N. Geisler, *Baker Encyclopedia of Christian Apologetics,* (Grand Rapids, Baker, 1999) 458.

As C. S. Lewis observed in his book *Miracles:*

Now of course we must agree with Hume that if there is absolutely "uniform experience" against miracles, if in other words they have never happened, why then they never have. Unfortunately we know the experience against them to be uniform only if we know that all the reports of them are false. And we can know all the reports to be false only if we know already that miracles have never occurred. In fact, we are arguing in a circle.[38]

Hume does not truly weigh evidence objectively; he simply adds up all the evidence against miracles. For example, death occurs over and over; but "…that a dead man should come to life…has never been observed in any age or country."[39] So even if there are reports of a miracle, according to Hume, we must reject them. In addition to the circular reasoning, there are problems with Hume's concept of adding up events to determine truth. Even if a few resurrections actually occurred, according to Hume's principles, one should not believe them.

Hume's faulty reasoning equates evidence with probability that it happened before. This is what C. S. Lewis calls "The majority vote of our past experience." He wrote, "The more often a thing has been known to happen, the more probable it is that it should happen again; and the less often the less probable."[40]

Hume does not weigh the quality of the evidence either. The claim by Mohammed that he was miraculously given the Koran

---

38   C. S. Lewis, *Miracles* (Glasgow, William Collins Sons,194) 106.

39   D. Hume, *An Enquiry Concerning Human Understanding,* ed. Eric Steinberg (Indianapolis, Hacket, 1993) 77.

40   C. S. Lewis, *Miracles,* 105.

a chapter at a time is almost infinitely removed from the claim of the apostle Paul that five hundred people saw the risen Christ and invited his critics to go speak with them[41]. Hume neglects that truth is not determined by majority vote. Here he is committing the "bandwagon" fallacy of arguing that something is true because it is believed (or should be) by most people (or most "wise" people).

According to this line of thinking, if one was genuinely dealt the perfect bridge hand, (which has happened) he should not believe it happened since the odds against it are over a thousand trillion to one. Norm Geisler writes:

> Sometimes the "odds" against an event are high (based on past observations of similar events), but the evidence for the event is very good (based on current observations or testimony for this event).[42]

Hume overlooks the reality that wise people base belief on facts, not just odds. When the odds against an event are high but the evidence is still very good, skepticism is unwarranted. By Hume's reasoning, one should eliminate belief in any unusual or unique event. If this line of reasoning were applied to history, unique historical events would be eliminated. Hume unwittingly encourages people to have irrational doubts about any event that occurs rarely.

It seems that in the end, Hume's argument "proves" too much. It proves that a person should not believe in a miracle even if it

---

41 See 1 Corinthians 15:6.

42 N. Geisler, *Baker Encyclopedia of Christian Apologetics,* (Grand Rapids, MI, Baker, 1999) 459.

does happen. This line of thought argues not that miracles do not occur, but that we should not believe they have occurred because the evidence shows how rare they actually are. How can you believe in a miracle if you must reject it because you have not seen it before? According to Geisler, "There is something patently absurd about claiming that an event should be disbelieved, even if one knows it happened."[43]

One of my friends has some training in philosophy, and he believes that only things that can be verified by sense experience (Empiricism) should be considered true. I asked him what he would do if a man predicted his own death, proceeded to die, his death was inarguably verified, and then he was seen alive after three days, and all of this happened in the presence of a number of witnesses, "including you," I said. "What if the dead man physically walked into the room at his own funeral?" I asked my friend. "Hypothetically speaking, what would you believe about what you saw?" His first response was that he would check himself into a mental hospital, but when I pressed him further, he finally admitted, "If a certifiably dead man showed up alive at his funeral, I guess I would have to change my worldview."

As my friend admitted this, he was by this admission, rejecting Hume's argument. Probability and evidence are not the same thing. And "wise" people ought to be open to examining not only their philosophical decisions, but also their evidence. Remember though, that the observer's prior worldview commitment may cause him to slight certain kinds of evidence.

---

43   Ibid.

I've addressed Hume's argument in some detail because it has been given such weight since the Enlightenment. The principal philosophical argument against the supernatural and the basis for much biblical criticism has been this argument. Now perhaps you are thinking that in this day and age, shouldn't we have more "scientific" arguments and concrete proofs against miracles? But science is impotent to make this sort of judgment. Modern science, or methodological Naturalism, is restricted to addressing only the natural world, acted upon only by natural forces. By definition then, *Materialists have no epistemological tool capable of addressing the supernatural.* Therefore Materialists can make *no* definitive statement about whether anything non-material can or cannot exist. So while the "proofs" against the supernatural have become louder and more dogmatic, they really haven't changed. Hume's fallacious argument has seen little improvement to this day.

At this point the reader might object that I've not dealt with the psychological argument that religious beliefs are mere projections or delusions based on wish fulfillment. Rather than go into Freud and others in detail, I will merely note that Anthony Flew, while still a prominent Atheist, cautioned his followers that the psychological argument cuts both ways. Belief projection counts against the Atheist as much as it does the Theist. It's easy to argue that Atheists deny God's existence out of a desire for personal autonomy, or perhaps the desire to kill their father! Thus, the psychological argument is a weak and often self-defeating argument for Atheists to use.

The Quest for the Historical Jesus

With the supposed demise of the supernatural during the age of reason, what was to be made of the Jesus found in the pages of the New Testament? Thomas Jefferson, an Enlightenment Deist, had an answer. He considered the Bible to be a good book and Jesus an exemplary ethical teacher. He advocated the study and public promulgation of the Bible, but only what he thought were the "real" teachings of Jesus. To fit his view, Jefferson produced what he first titled "The Philosophy of Jesus of Nazareth," according to a *Wall Street Journal* article written by Stephen Prothero. And what did Jefferson do with the supernatural? Simple: he cut it out—literally. Sometime in 1804, Jefferson sat down with two Bibles and one razor, and removed the miraculous parts of the New Testament, hoping the remainder would be the historical and ethical Jesus. But this artificial separation yields complete nonsense, and as Prothero wrote "...not a hint of the resurrection."[44] Today it seems that the so-called scholars of the Jesus Seminar are still using a similar approach by making sweeping announcements claiming that Christian beliefs and doctrines are just superstitious nonsense, echoing Jefferson from over two hundred years ago.

The modern history of Jesus studies can be divided into three periods or quests. The first quest was an early nineteenth century attempt to cast Jesus into various roles that reflected the romanticized projections of its authors—usually into some form of a simple Jewish teacher. But in 1835, in response to German theologian

---

44 S. Prothero "Thomas Jefferson's Cut-and-Paste Bible." *Wall Street Journal*, March 25, 2011, WSJ.com

Schleiermacher's book *The Life of Jesus,* David Strauss wrote his critique titled *The Christ of Faith and the Jesus of History.* Strauss argued that the gospels were mythological and that the historical Jesus could not be found in them. Strauss thought that to actually be true to Jesus' teaching, we needed to "...rid ourselves of the idea of a supernatural Christ."[45] Like Jefferson before him, Strauss' arguments were based on little more than an anti-supernatural bias.

What followed in biblical writing was an attempt to separate what the apostles said about Jesus from what Jesus actually said about himself. This partition between the "Christ of faith" and the "Jesus of history" remains a tenant of liberal New Testament research. It is rooted in the erroneous idea that since the gospels contain theology, they cannot contain history. The mistake is to consider theology and history to be mutually exclusive. Theological does not mean non-historical.

While we noted earlier that science is impotent to investigate non-material causes, the same cannot be said of history and the events in the New Testament (NT). Christianity claims to be a historical religion, in which a transcendent, supernatural God acts in time and space. This God actually does things that make a difference. The claimed events are open, in principle, to historical investigation. Historians too have biases and methodologies. Once they are disclosed, as an honest historian will do, they can be evaluated as to how suitable they will be for the task at hand. The problems of reconstructing the past are well known, but most historians are historical realists, meaning

---

45 D. Strauss, *The Christ of Faith and the Jesus of History*, trans. Leander Keck, (Philadelphia, Fortress, 1977) 161.

that past reality can, to some meaningful degree, be recovered. If it could not, they would be out of a job. Liberal theologians, to the extent they understand historical methodology at all, tend to be historic skeptics. They often make historical claims person relative or observer dependent just as they tend to do with religious truth ("It's true for me."). The interesting outcome is that the historian is often far less skeptical about the NT's ability to transmit historical fact than the theologian. This is something to keep in mind when evaluating their assessments.

Albert Schweitzer brought this period to a close in 1906 with his *The Quest for the Historical Jesus*. To his credit, he pointed out the futility of painting Jesus into one role or another on rationalistic schemes based on some modern category. Schweitzer brings together the scholarship of the best of the German higher critics' distillation of the so-called "gloss" and "redaction" of verses of the gospels and removes what he believes are the historical words of Jesus—but only to paint a picture of a misguided teacher trying to usher in the kingdom of God by Jesus' own martyrdom on a Roman cross.

According to Schweitzer,

The Messiahship of Jesus, as we find it in the gospels, is a product of early Christian theology correcting history according to its own conceptions.[46]

The majority of writers at the end of the nineteenth century were casting Jesus into the role of an ideal hero of the Christian

---

46 A. Schweitzer, *The Quest of the Historical Jesus,* trans. W. Montgomery (New York, Macmillan, 1950), 338.

community, and Schweitzer noted that from the socio-religious standpoint, this "figure of *The Christ*" [emphasis added] is a "sublimation of religious expression" and the Christian celebration of a Lord's supper was "The memorial feast of this Ideal Hero."[47] Yet after pointing this out, Schweitzer does exactly the same thing that he criticized in others by portraying Jesus as a deluded doomsayer.

Schweitzer was correct in calling previous quests for the historical Jesus misguided, but he promptly fell into the same trap. He argued that Jesus' message was eschatological in nature, meaning Jesus thought he was ushering in the end of the world. The King James Bible translates Jesus as speaking of the end of the world (Matthew 24:3), but a more correct translation from the Greek manuscripts would read "end of the age," which most biblical scholars today believe refers to the end of the old covenant based on the law of Moses.

Schweitzer goes on to say that Jesus was misguided and delusional, allowing himself to be put on the cross to usher in the end of the world. This claim has two problems. The first is that it denies Schweitzer's major premise. If the historical Jesus is not recoverable, how could he have recovered this bit of information? Further, C. S. Lewis, in his "lord, liar, lunatic" conundrum took on the "delusional" argument.[48] Psychohistory is a dubious endeavor, but most who have looked at the matter seriously say that Jesus offers a picture of sanity and self-control.

---

47   Ibid., 317.

48   C. S. Lewis, *Mere Christianity* (San Francisco, Harper Collins, 2001), 52.

Jesus' cry to his father on the cross is traditional Christian theology that has nothing to do with delusions, and in fact was an apparently intentional reference on Jesus' part to an Old Testament prophecy. Schweitzer would have been more credible if he'd said that the apostles or the church made up the whole story. The accusation that Jesus was delusional can be dismissed for lack of evidence and incongruity with the rest of the text.

This brings us to the second part of the quest for the historical Jesus, when the quest devolved into total skepticism. During this time, some wanted to salvage Christianity by taking another route. Rudolf Bultmann led this attempt in the 1930s. Interestingly, Bultmann did not think we could know anything of the life and personality of Jesus. In this sense he follows Schweitzer but avoids Schweitzer's error of then making claims about what he had claimed was not knowable. In his writings, Bultmann claims that early Christian sources show no interest in Jesus' life and personality, and that the material is basically legendary. Bultmann is imposing modern standards of biography on an ancient text. Biographical material from that era simply did not spend much time worrying about issues like, "How did you feel about your childhood?" In his attempt to save Christianity, Bultmann moves from historical inquiry to existential encounter; he continues the demythologizing started by Strauss—the German theologian who started the first quest to find the historical Jesus—with the argument that in the age of the electric light bulb and the radio, how can anyone believe in miracles? (I will not comment on the absurdity of this argument.) In an essay entitled "Crisis in Belief," Bultmann wrote that *real* belief in God is "...*not a general truth*" [emphasis in the original] and that *weltanshauung* (or worldview) is "...in sharpest contrast to belief in God."[49]

Rejecting the reliability of the gospels, Bultmann asks people to generate faith in Christ out of pure desire and with no basis in fact. Existentialism is the attempt to find meaning in an uncaring and meaningless universe; the Existentialist "leaps" for a fabricated reality. I realize this is a gross oversimplification and that there are more sophisticated and nuanced forms of Existentialism. But encountering a Christ of faith based on an unknowable Jesus seems like self-delusion and is hardly an improvement on the "mythology" Bultmann is trying to eliminate in his attempt to be more scientific.

In contrast to the prior trends, the so-called new or third quest is not as skeptical about recovering something from history, but it is also home to a radical tradition exemplified by the Jesus Seminar member, Bishop John Shelby Spong, and others. In part, they base their work on the gospel of Thomas and other Gnostic "gospels" (spiritualized, non-historical accounts), as well as so-called "Q" material. When you turn on your television for that typical Easter special, a Jesus Seminar scholar will be called on to tell America that most of the things traditionally believed about Jesus never happened. Helping facilitate this viewpoint, certain media wish to mainstream the Jesus Seminar, a self-styled group consisting of about 200 activists, of which only a handful have scholarly credentials. Even among non-Christian scholars, the Jesus Seminar

---

49   R. Bultmann, *Essays: Philosophical and Theological* (London, SCM Press, 1955) 7-8.

is at the radical fringe of NT studies but is the face that seems favored by much of the media.

But what of the Jesus Seminar's claims?

First, using the gospel of Thomas as a source document is ridiculous. In spite of its historical inaccuracy, the gospel of Thomas is popular because Gnosticism (think New Age religion) is currently popular. Gnosticism is what you find in *The Da Vinci Code* and is based on a collection of "gospels" written at least a hundred years after the traditional ones. A casual read will show they are nothing like the traditional canonical gospels, and are gospels in name only. They make no attempt to convey actual history. Why a NT scholar would prefer a source far removed from the original documents indicates how far the Jesus Seminar is willing to go to push its agenda.

Second, the so-called Q document is hypothetical. Technically, Q (*quelle*, the word *source* in German), are the sayings common to Matthew and Luke that are not found in Mark.[50] Because these gospels share certain material that is essentially the same, the theory is that there must have been a precursor source document, referred to as Q, that has been lost, but from which both Matthew and Luke shared material. Although this theory is supported by biblical scholarship, understand that there is no Q document in existence, and as Craig Blomberg writes "...there has been an entire cottage industry of studies on the hypothetical Q-document..."[51] The

---

50   C. Blomberg. *The Historical Reliability of the Gospels, 2nd ed.*(Downers Grove, IL, InterVarsity Press, 2007), 39.

51   Ibid., 44.

most that can be said about this possible source is that Matthew and Luke were using a common tradition (possibly Mark + Q) and expanded on the rough and ready style of Mark (or, in Matthew's case, added to first-hand experience) Luke says in his prologue that he is using sourced material, obtained by interviewing eyewitnesses. But the rationalistic schemes of the Jesus Seminar go far beyond the obvious. The Seminar claims this material represents the earliest stratum of what makes up the gospel tradition so it's the most reliable part. Their reasoning is that these sayings, or quotes, of Jesus contain no supernatural material. Since the Jesus Seminar knows nothing supernatural really happened, they conclude that these sayings must therefore represent the earliest and most accurate material. But this is arguing in a circle—the scholars know the sayings (Q) are early and reliable because they contain no recounting of miracles. Then they say they know no miracles happened because they are not in the earliest and most reliable material! The mysterious Q, supposedly an early, non-supernatural gospel reflecting the true Jesus, is a figment of liberal scholarship.

The current widespread promotion of Gnostic/New Age religion has produced a whole genre of popular books that try to turn Jesus into some sort of Far Eastern guru. But whatever else Jesus is, the religions of the Far East have no claim on him. He is a product of Judaism. The current third quest is beginning to study Jesus as a Jew. Tom Wright, in his book *Who is Jesus?*, sums up these quests as follows: "the Old Quest up to Schweitzer dug a massive ditch dividing the historical Jesus from the Christ of faith. After Schweitzer, the ditch remained unfilled and any attempt at connecting the real Jesus with the faith of his followers was promptly demolished. But since about the nineteen sixties, the mood of skepticism has lifted because theologians have found it harder to ignore the historical method, especially as it applies to the NT. "This historical perspective requires looking at Jesus as he saw himself—as the predicted Jewish Messiah. To the extent that he exceeds Judaism, he does so, on his own, without the influence of other philosophies or world religions.

By looking at the NT as a first century Jewish document, we can put away the popular misconception that it was the creation of a later Greco-Roman Church. Indeed, a Jewish lens is appropriate for NT scholarship, and no other makes sense of Jesus studies because without knowing where we came from, we have no way to evaluate where we are. Scholars have been culturally captive of their own time and creating a Jesus of their own minds. In all its 300-year history, the rigid anti-miracle camp in NT studies has never been able to properly understand the NT. In asking the question, why did the NT writers write this stuff, they never consider the obvious: *perhaps it really happened.*

God's Existence and the Resurrection of Jesus

• • •

S o far, we've seen two arguments for the existence of God. The cosmological argument asserts that there is a Creator who is separate from the universe itself. The argument from design shows that the observable properties of the natural world suggest overwhelmingly that intelligence intervened in the universe's creation and is evident at other points, most clearly in the creation of life from non-life. It is this intervention in the natural world that would seem to permit another class of "nature miracles," or events that cannot be explained by the closed chain of cause and effect required by Naturalism. Most scientists hate this alleged tinkering by God because at this point they have lost control. Even scientists that believe in God think it is somehow beneath God to have to revisit his work. A really skilled pool player could put all the balls in the pocket in one shot! But this misunderstands what it means to violate a law of nature. If I drop an apple, natural law says it should hit the floor. But what happens if I catch it? Has a law been broken? If I am a free agent, a powerful intuition that most of us have, then what I have demonstrated is mind over matter. Is it a violation of nature? Not in the sense of agent causation, but it would definitely be a sign.

These are the kinds of events in the Bible that are reported by observation. They could be clearly identified by the observers. For example, the parting of the Red Sea (probably the Gulf of Aquaba or some lake in the Nile Delta) or Jesus walking on water: these are reports from observation. The Hebrews did not have a category for miracle as God was behind everything except human freedom. But they could distinguish these things as signs and were not as gullible as moderns think. They knew the normal operations of nature and where babies came from. The point is they could identify signs. These were not random misunderstandings because they occurred in the context of other events. It is one thing for lightning to strike and to call it "god." It is quite another for the Prophet Elijah to call down fire in a contest with Pagans and it happens. I realize this has no evidential value for skeptics, to whom it is just a reported story. But what if there was a miracle so well attested to, only a David Hume-type skeptic could argue against it?

In the last chapter we took up the problem of miracles in general and showed there is no good reason to exclude them *a priori*. Christians focus most directly on the miracle of Jesus' resurrection. Even former leading Atheist philosopher Antony Flew, who withheld belief in miracles as understood in the Bible (even as he came to advocate for design in the universe) said that the resurrection of Jesus is the best-supported example of a miracle in all of human history.

The existence of God does not require the resurrection, but the resurrection points to the existence of God. This is not just because it is unusual, as Hume would put it, but also because Jesus' radical claims to divinity would not likely be vindicated by a God that disputed those claims or just wasn't paying attention.

Pantheists, who hold that god is everything and everything is god, have an entirely different take on the resurrection and miracles in general. Pantheists believe that everything that happens in the universe is natural and that nature itself is god. They say that Jesus was just a man who realized the divine power within him—the same divine power that is within all of us. Thus, Jesus' enlightened status is proved by his mastery of nature. According to this reasoning, we all have the potential to raise ourselves from the dead if only we become sufficiently enlightened. Oprah gurus Eckhart Tolle and Deepak Chopra have popularized ideas from Eastern religion. This is an easy sell to the public. People have wanted to be "like God" since the serpent first sold the idea to Eve and Adam. Until they can first be disabused of their worldview, no amount of evidence for the resurrection will drive Pantheists to a true understanding of Christianity, and they will never believe that Jesus is the *unique* son of God.

The cosmological argument falsifies Pantheism. Pantheism requires some form of an eternal (or oscillating/reincarnating) universe and the cosmological argument refutes the existence of such a universe. Time is not circular as in Pantheism but has a beginning, according to science and the Bible.

The Pantheist can offer no evidence to show that his or her worldview is true; it's just a philosophical idea. It's important to note that Jesus himself, whom Pantheists hold to be an enlightened great teacher, neither promoted Pantheism nor suggested in any way that humans can self-realize their personal divinity. On the contrary, Jesus was a strict Jewish Monotheist who had the audacity to openly declare himself, and only himself, to be of the same substance as God.

Concerning Naturalism, I once watched Michael Shermer of *Skeptic* magazine as he sat on a panel discussing religion. There was also a Christian on the panel, and Shermer demanded a detailed *physical* explanation of how Jesus rose from the dead. Of course, this was not possible because there is no *natural* way that anyone can come back from the dead. Shermer was asking for something that his worldview simply could not accommodate. But again, if the cosmological and design arguments hold, Naturalism must be false. As a result, Shermer's objections to the resurrection do not need to be answered in naturalistic terms until he somehow proves that his worldview is at least more plausible than Theism.

If the case for Naturalism is sufficiently weakened by the cosmological and design arguments, as I am convinced is the case, and the resurrection is sufficiently attested, we are in a position to argue that God raised Jesus from the dead. From this foundation I will present an argument that Jesus' resurrection is best explained by the existence of a personal God (Theism).

Because the arguments for the resurrection are historical, two common objections arise at this juncture.

One objection is that history is essentially unknowable. This is the postmodern idea that history—"a grand metanarrative"— is written by the winners. Liberal theologians like to argue that the earliest strains of Christianity were not supernatural. They say that multiple factions of Christianity fought it out with each other and that the strongest faction—the Paul party, named for St. Paul and his brand of Christianity—won out. Others say that the idea of a physical resurrection came through a process of mythological development. Still another, that seems to be in fashion right now, is that the early Christians borrowed ideas like virgin birth and resurrection from the many so-called mystery religions and cults that were flourishing in the late first and second centuries. The problem here is that most of these cults post-date the NT. Any borrowing of ideas about resurrection was from Christianity by the other cults, not the other way around. Second, the similarities of the NT to the fertility cults of Paganism, with its dying and rising gods, are weak to nonexistent. These gods were tied to weather patterns and crop cycles, while the NT is rooted in Old Testament prophecy. Third, the early Christians were monotheistic Jews with a history of fierce separation from Paganism for over four hundred years.

Another skeptical view is that the early Catholic Church created the resurrection story for doctrinal purposes or political control. Some place this alleged conspiracy as late as the Council of Nicaea in 325 AD under the direction of Constantine. Dan Brown in *The Da Vinci Code* internationally peddled this erroneous viewpoint. All of these arguments can be swept aside if it can be shown that belief in the resurrection was firm in the minds of Jesus' earliest followers—his disciples—and other eyewitnesses who were alive within one generation of the resurrection. I will present detailed dating arguments later.

A second, and related, objection concerns skepticism about past events. Most historians are quite certain about the events during first century Roman history. In their minds, the essentials of the lives of the Roman emperors are solidly established. Yet some of these same people maintain a deep skepticism about the historical accounts found in the NT. This is in spite of the fact that—based on the number of copies of NT manuscripts and the proximity of these copies to the actual dates of the events (textual attestation)—the NT is far more reliable than *any* writings from secular history. Scholars do not doubt the truth of the secular writings, so this pervasive skepticism towards the NT amounts to the same anti-supernatural bias we've seen in other areas like cosmology and design. A well-entrenched worldview is a difficult thing to overcome.

Skeptics claim that the followers of Jesus were not reliable because they had a religious agenda. Of course Jesus' followers had an agenda, but the agenda was caused by the events—not the other way around. The reason Roman and Jewish historians did not give a detailed account of Jesus (though there is significant material from these sources) is that this was just not a major event for the Roman Empire at that time. Likewise the NT writers did not write much about Rome since it was not their purpose. However, enough historical context exists in the NT to firmly connect it to specific times and locations. Luke, who is recognized as a careful researcher ("…having investigated everything from the beginning…")[52], gives abundant historical material in the book of Acts. To reject Luke's

---

52   See Luke 1:3.

highly accurate historical markers because it is tied to religion is just a willful disregard of the facts.

Regardless of their faiths and whether or not they believe in the resurrection, most NT scholars and most secular historians attest to the historical truth of Jesus' existence and the historical facts concerning the resurrection. NT scholar Gary Habermas has compiled what over 2000 NT scholars hold as certain or probable minimum facts concerning the resurrection:[53]

1. Jesus died on a Roman cross sometime between 30 and 33 AD.

2. He was buried in a tomb owned by Joseph of Arimathea, a member of the Jewish high council who was a well-known figure at the time. It's unlikely that the character of Joseph of Arimathea would be invented since he was on the wrong side of the Christian case. Just such a person would have had the connections to obtain the body from Pilate.

3. The tomb was found empty on "the first day of the week" (Easter morning), the third day after Jesus' crucifixion according to Jewish counting. The reason it was empty is, of course, hotly debated.

4. Jesus' followers sincerely believed that they saw, ate with, physically touched, and talked with Jesus throughout the forty days after the resurrection and prior to his ascension. The cause of this belief also remains a subject of debate.

---

53 See G. Habermas & M. Licona, *The Case for the Resurrection of Jesus* (Grand Rapids, MI, Kregel, 2004).

5. The actions of Jesus' followers, as orthodox Jews, and the founding of the early Church at Pentecost, fifty days after the resurrection (see Acts 2 in the NT) can only be explained by numbers three and four in this list.

Putting aside anti-supernatural bias, by far the best explanation for this set of generally accepted facts is that God raised Jesus from the dead. If this sounds like a leap, it must be noted that it is the only theory that accounts for all the facts, including the subsequent actions of his followers for the next forty years. Every naturalistic theory fails to account for one or more of the facts or resorts to some form of special pleading such as Jesus had a twin brother. Previous naturalistic theories to account for the resurrection (Jesus merely swooned and therefore didn't really die on the cross, the women all went to the wrong tomb on Easter morning, all five hundred of the disciples hallucinated the appearances, etc.) no longer have standing among most academics. Most counterarguments are based mainly on philosophical presuppositions and (faith-based) worldview commitments rather than on historical evidence.[54]

---

54 One well-known academic, Bart Ehrman, appeals to the unreliability of the text. Ehrman dedicated his work to his professor, Bruce Metzger at Princeton. Interestingly Dr Metzger, the dean of textual critics, did believe the NT was reliably transmitted. Ehrman lost his faith over a possible error in Mark's gospel. While this may count against the doctrine of biblical inerrancy, an in-house debate, it hardly counts against the general reliability of the NT. His methodology, while technically accurate, far overstates his case. He counts spelling variations as "errors." Many of the "problems" he "discovers" are already footnoted in most modern Bible translations. His fundamentalist past colors his take on what the Bible should look like.

The hypothesis, "God raised Jesus from the dead" far exceeds all competing hypotheses in explanatory scope and power—the number of facts and the ability to explain those facts that are agreed on by most scholars. It also confirms that the God of the universe is the Judeo-Christian God.

Is the New Testament Historically Reliable?

● ● ●

B efore trusting what the NT says about Jesus, it is imperative to evaluate whether it is historically reliable. The question of its historicity must be broken down into several parts:

1. How closely does the current text match the original(s)?

2. When was it written and who wrote it? This addresses the crucial question of whether the NT's authors were in a position to know the truth about the events they recorded.

3. Did the authors present a factual account of the events? If the authors were in a position to know the truth, then a critic of the NT is forced to charge the authors with having lied and subsequently explain why they did not tell the truth. But if the evidence firmly suggests the authors *did not* lie, it makes sense to trust the NT's accounts about Jesus. Surely one is justified in doing so.

We addressed the first question earlier by noting that the NT is by far the best-attested book in all of antiquity. By this we mean that we have the most copies from the earliest dates as compared to any other ancient work (such as *The Iliad*). This fact has been established through the science of textual criticism, where approximately five thousand early manuscripts were compared for similarities and differences. The conclusion of textual scholars is that we have recovered over 98% of what the original authors wrote. No significant teaching or doctrine is affected by the 2% variant.

HISTORICAL EVIDENCE ABOUT THE NEW TESTAMENT

• • •

T he question of when the original documents were written is the key to NT reliability. The answer will tell us whether the NT contains eyewitness material. While the gospels are a combination of history, teaching, and theology and the epistles (letters from the apostles) are letters of instruction, the book of Acts is the history of the early Church from its first weeks to the early 60s AD. By claiming many historical details, Acts is subject to external verification. For this reason early twentieth century British archaeologist, Sir Ramsey, decided to attack the NT by checking the historical details of Acts. To his surprise, Luke's account perfectly matched with the historical facts as best they could be determined from extra-biblical sources. As a result of the unexpected outcome of his investigation he became a Christian.

The NT's points of contact with the pre-70 AD Roman world are too many to enumerate here. But for dating purposes, the general line of reasoning goes like this: Peter and Paul are alive at the end of the book of Acts. Paul is still under house arrest, and according to John McRay, that occurred sometime during 57-59AD.[55] We know from external sources that Peter and Paul died under Caesar

---

55   J. McRay, *Paul: His Life and Teaching* (Grand Rapids, Baker, 2003), 73-70.

Nero in 68. Therefore Acts was probably written before the mid-60s. Also in Acts there was no hint of trouble with the Romans; the Jewish leadership was making most of the complaints about Christians, especially about Paul.

An additional early dating argument for the NT can be seen in an interesting quote found in Paul's first epistle to Timothy, dated by John McRay to around 65 AD, which agrees with Craig Blomberg's date range of sometime during 63 to 67 AD.[56] Most scholars agree that in 1 Timothy 5:18 are quotes from both Deuteronomy 25:4 and Luke 10:7, where the passage written by Paul reads "For the scripture says, 'You shall not muzzle an ox when it treads out the grain,' and, 'the laborer deserves his wages.'" Kostenberger and Kruger write of the formulation of the two scripture references "… both citations bear the same authoritative scriptural status."[57] So it would seem that we have Luke's gospel treated as authoritative at or before 63 AD.

Scholars recognize a literary dependency among the first three gospels (Matthew, Mark, and Luke). The bulk of the material in Mark's account is also contained within Matthew and Luke, hence most modern scholars consider Mark to have been written first, although Christian tradition has maintained from the early second century that Matthew wrote first. Noted Rabbi Gamaliel is quoted in a literary tale dated by some scholars from 72 AD, where this

---

56 C. Blomberg, *From Pentecost to Patmos* (Nashville, TN, B & H Academic, 2006), 348.

57 A. Kostenberger and M. Kruger, *Heresy of Orthodoxy: How Contemporary Culture's Fascination with Diversity has Reshaped Our Understanding of Early Christianity,* (Wheaton, IL, Crossways, 2010), 129.

parody of Matthew's gospel is found within the Talmud (Jewish commentary) is found. Gamaliel died around 50 AD, about twenty years before the Romans destroyed Jerusalem;[58] so by simple logic, this would push Matthew back to the 40s or earlier, less than twenty years after the events it describes, something no scholar would have dared to imagine until recently. It would also support the claim of the church fathers that Matthew wrote first.

Mark's gospel also has clues to its early date. One such clue is that Mark refers to the high priest involved in Jesus' crucifixion without naming him, which strongly implies that Mark's audience knew his name: Caiaphas. Since Caiaphas is known to have died seven years after the crucifixion, Mark's passion material, which refers to the high priest, must have been sourced very close to the event—so close that Mark assumes his audience knows it is the current high priest. Many scholars believe Mark's passion material comes from Peter. The important point is that it reflects what the early church believed in the first few years after the crucifixion.

What does all this mean? It overwhelmingly points to a fixed Christian tradition that was already established within a few years following the events described in the NT and a date of finished work before the destruction of the great temple in 70 AD.

Hardly anyone doubts the authenticity of Paul's major epistles; like Romans, 1 and 2, Corinthians, and Galatians. They have been dated by reference to a Roman proconsul, Gallio, who probably

---

58   N. Altman, "Talmud Confirms an Early Gospel of Matthew," *Toronto Star,* December 13, 2003. http://search.ebscohost.com/login.aspx?direct=true&db=nf h&AN=6FP3182224561&site=ehost-live

began his term in office in May of 51 AD,[59] before whom Paul was brought that same year (Acts 18:15).[60] Paul's detailed message on the resurrection in 1 Corinthians 15:3-5 (written about 53 AD) says, "What I received I passed on to you as of first importance…"[61] This may seem unremarkable, but Paul used the technical language of a pre-Christian rabbi, for whom "passed on" means "received tradition." This shows that his resurrection tradition pre-dated Paul and reflects the care taken in passing along oral traditions with precision. According to Craig Blomberg "…there is every reason to believe that many of the sayings and actions of Jesus would have been very carefully safeguarded in the first decades of the church's history…"[62] further strengthening the early dating of the gospel accounts.

Additionally a general dating argument can be made concerning the entire NT. By 70 AD, Jerusalem and the Jewish temple had been completely destroyed by the Romans. Not one stone was left standing, just as Jesus had predicted. Most skeptics have attempted to date the formation of the NT later than 70 AD because it eliminates not only most of the eyewitness testimony but also the embarrassing problem of Jesus having predicted the destruction of the temple in the first three gospels—an obvious prophetic miracle. For this sect of Judaism—which is what early Christianity was—failing to mention the destruction of the center of Jewish life

---

59   J. McRay. *Paul: His Life and Teaching,* (Grand Rapids, MI, Baker, 2003), 76.

60   Ibid., 76.

61   *New International Version,* (Colorado Springs, International Bible Society, 1984).

62   C. Blomberg. *The Historical Reliability of the Gospels, 2nd ed.* (Downers Grove, IL., InterVarsity Press, 2007), 62.

would be unthinkable. Matthew, with his emphasis on prophecy and fulfillment for his mostly Jewish audience, records Jesus predicting the destruction of the temple. If the Matthew account had been written after the destruction in 70 AD, not saying, "It was fulfilled" would be completely inconsistent with his style. With an early parody of Matthew combined with the testimony of the early church fathers, it seems unbelievable that the generally accepted date for Matthew would be 80 AD. For Matthew to be writing after the destruction of the temple and not mention it would be like a text on United States history neglecting to mention the Civil War. Though some final editing and arranging may have taken place after 70 AD, the Christian tradition must have been firmly fixed by that time. It is clear that the late date theories by critics of the NT are without warrant.

This evidence also dispenses with theories that the NT was born through the accretion of myth and legend. According to Roman historian A. N. Sherman-White, when you compare how we look at well-attested histories, (e.g., Herodias) using the form-criticism method on a set of histories written down from oral tradition "Forty to seventy years later, after they had been remodeled by at least one generation…"[63] you still find the truth. As Sherman-White states:

> Herodias enables us to test the tempo of myth-making, and the tests suggest that even two generations are too short a span to allow the mythical tendency to prevail over the hard historic core of the oral tradition.[64]

---

63   A. N. Sherwin-White, *Roman Society and Roman Law in the New Testament.* (UK, Oxford University Press, 1963), 189.

64   Ibid., 190.

The conclusion of this scholar of Roman history is that we have more confidence in the historical accuracy in the NT, not less. In Sherman-White's words:

> It is astonishing that the historical Christ is unknowable and the history of his mission cannot be written. This seems very curious when one compares the case for the best-known contemporary of Christ, who like Christ is a well-documented figure—Tiberius Caesar.[65]

Who Wrote the New Testament?

Surprisingly, this is not of critical importance. Whether the first gospel in the NT is only according to Matthew or in Matthew's own hand does not reflect on its reliability. Luke is clearly identified by Paul as a companion in 2 Timothy 4:11. Paul and Peter both write in their own name. Peter refers to Paul's writing as "difficult to understand" (2 Peter 3:16), but Peter considered it inspired scripture. All NT writers either knew each other directly or had another apostle in common. Though it can't be fully proven, there is little reason to doubt the traditional authorship of most of the NT books. Only the book of Hebrews remains of unknown authorship. Yet it is undoubtedly from Paul's inner circle, though probably not by him as was thought by the translators of the King James Bible. The crucial fact to remember is that the books come from persons in a position to know the facts.

The first and second generations after the apostles make many references to apostolic writings. Polycarp was a disciple of John,

---

65   Ibid., 187.

and Iranaius, whose writings we know, learned about John from Polycarp. In fact, if the entire NT were lost, it could be reconstructed entirely from post-apostolic writings of the church fathers, who quoted heavily from the NT writers.

The vast majority of scholars consider Paul's writings authentic, though some disagreement remains about some of the shorter personal letters. However, the use of secretaries was common, and Paul even indicates where he writes by his own hand or is using a scribe. A de facto canon, or established set of authoritative writings, was essentially in place by the end of the first century AD. The epistle of 1 Clement (not part of the NT), written by Clement, a prominent leader in Rome who heard Peter's preaching, was circulated in the Christian community around 95 AD. In this epistle are numerous references to Paul's letters, and according to Kostenberger and Kruger, "...numerous gospel citations...that seem to come from Matthew and Luke (and possibly Mark), and some scholars have noted allusions to Acts, James, and 1 Peter."[66] And if one reads the epistle written by Polycarp you see similar references. As Kostenberger and Kruger have concluded:

> In the end, with these considerations in mind, Polycarp provides a noteworthy confirmation of the trend...By a very early point—in this case around AD 110—New Testament books were not only called but were also functioning as authoritative scripture...[I]t is reasonable to think that his [Polycarp's] beliefs concerning the canon of scripture would be fairly widespread by this time.[67]

---

66 A. Kostenberger and M. Kruger, *The Heresy of Orthodoxy*, (Wheaton, IL, Crossway, 2010), 139.

67 Ibid., 145.

Even with the rise of the so-called apocryphal or false gospels, which began to appear around 150 AD, the early church knew of these other writings, and had no question about what books belonged as scripture. Early Christians were not willing to accept books as canon written past the apostolic age. According to Kostenberger and Kruger, by the beginning of the second century, the canon was considered closed; this was long before the Council of Nicaea in 325 AD. The fact that all the books of the NT were carefully analyzed shows the great care the early church took with its accepted material and how clearly early Christianity understood its theological convictions.[68]

To look specifically at the gospels, Luke (dating from about 60 AD) was really the first investigative reporter. Though he was apparently not an eyewitness himself, he clearly states that he interviewed eyewitnesses to come up with an accurate account of the events that he was transcribing. The accuracy of his historical work is considered unmatched in antiquity. And when you read the apostle John—in his own material—he keeps appealing, "This is written so that you may believe." John also wrote the book of Revelation, which refers to the temple in the present tense, which indicates a pre-70 AD date. Mark's gospel is the least polished; this reflects the tradition that Mark was a transcriber of very early events recounted by Peter; Mark's literary skills would have been rudimentary at that time. While the NT was written in common Greek, the language suggests translation from the Hebrew or Aramaic of the mid-first century.

---

68 Ibid., 170-71.

Many theoretical, scholarly debates remain ongoing about which writer borrowed what from whom, but in the end it's clear that they were all working with similar eyewitness material. The arguments presented here, while brief, collapse the criticism that the NT is merely the product of religious imagination. The scholarship shows that it is clearly grounded in history. The remaining refuge of the skeptic has to be enlightenment anti-supernatural bias, or the very recent tendency of postmodern thought to make all experience person-relative and hence, not objective.

Jesus' Self-Understanding

Many critics today say that Jesus never claimed to be God. While we have no record that he used those *exact* words, his claims were unmistakable to first century Jews.

During their early ministry, Jesus and John the Baptist preached that the kingdom of God had arrived. Jesus avoided direct Messianic claims so as not to precipitate too soon the events that would lead to his death. Jesus' most popular title for himself is "the son of man." To a modern reader, this may sound like a human title, but in fact Jesus was referring to the son of man in Daniel 7 from the Old Testament—this son of man is seated at the right hand of God the father. Obviously, this is a strong claim—one that would be unmistakable to his audience, who were quite familiar with the book of Daniel.

In the northern region of Caesarea Philippi, Jesus asked his disciples, "Who do people say the son of man is?" They replied, "Some say John the Baptist, others say Elijah, and still others

Jeremiah, or one of the prophets." Jesus then directed the question back to the disciples: "What about you?" he asked, "Who do you say that I am?" Peter answered, "You are the Christ, the son of the living God." Jesus replied, "You are blessed, Simon son of John because my father in heaven has revealed this to you. You did learn this from any human being." (Matthew 16:13-16; Mark 8:27-30; Luke 9:18-20)

Here Jesus makes a strong claim to be the *Christ*, which is the Greek term for *Messiah*, meaning "God's anointed"—the long-awaited Jewish deliverer. However, Jesus then referred to "my father in heaven." No Jew would ever refer to Yahweh (YHWH), the sacred covenant name of God, as his father. Today we may read these words lightly, but to a first century Jew, they would have been an unimaginable claim, in fact a blasphemous claim of divinity that could get a Jew executed.

Additionally, Jesus *accepted* worship, something only God could receive. He also claimed to forgive sins, a prerogative of God alone. He tried to conceal this from the religious leaders, knowing that it would help provide the impetus for his arrest, which he wanted to delay until the right time. Jesus even claimed the right to alter the Torah, the Jewish law, which was written by God himself.

At his trial before the high priest, Jesus called himself the "I AM" of Exodus 20, which is the Jewish covenant name of God. YHWH means quite literally "I am that I am." This is the name God called himself when asked by Moses at the burning bush (Exodus 3:13-15). During the examination before the Sanhedrin, the high priest tore his robes, a sign of indignation prescribed by the Jewish council for cases of blasphemy (see Matthew 26:65 and Mark 14:63). The sentence for claiming to be God was unequivocal—death—a sentence they carried out as quickly as possible. Caiaphas knew exactly what Jesus meant by these words.

These strong claims within the historically accurate text of the NT must be accounted for. C. S. Lewis sets this up as the famous "lord, liar, lunatic" conundrum.[69] The only way to account for Jesus' self claims is that Jesus was (1) a lunatic and delusional, (2) he was a deceitful liar; or (3) that he was and is the lord God. But there is nothing in his words to indicate that he was deceitful, and he maintained extreme self-control. Modern scholars try to get around Lewis' so-called "trilemma" by adding a fourth "L," for legend. We dealt with this last possibility in the previous material on eyewitness testimony, so the legend argument can be dismissed. The only reasonable conclusion is that Jesus must be who he claimed to be! God validated his outrageous claims by raising him from the dead.

If this is Jesus' self-understanding as recorded by his disciples, then they must have accepted this understanding in light of the resurrection. The true church has always held to this. There were never any alternate Christianities, then or now.

A Funny Thing Happened on the Road to Damascus

A "road to Damascus experience" is a common expression for a life-changing event.

Saul of Tarsus was probably the number two Jewish religious authority after Gamaliel. He was so zealous for his religion that

---

69 See C.S. Lewis, *Mere Christianity* (San Francisco, HarperCollins, 1952), 52.

he made it his mission to stamp out this new cult called "The Way." With letters of authority from the high council, he went to Damascus with a band of thugs to kill or put in prison as many members of the nascent church as possible. On the road he met Jesus in the form of a brilliant light and a voice. This was not the human body of the post resurrection appearances as Jesus had already ascended to heaven. His companions saw the light but did not hear the voice, which spoke to Saul in his own language. You can read the rest of the story in Acts 9. It's repeated twice more in Acts and referred to by Paul in his letters.

On a bit of an aside, Saul did not change his name after his conversion, but he had always had both the name Saul (*Saulos* in Greek); Paul (*Paulos*) was his Roman *cognomen*, or second name. But according to John McRay, Paul would change the use of his name according to the company he was keeping. This is consistent with his letters in which he uses his Roman name due to his mainly Gentile audience.[70]

As Paul wrote in his letter to the church he founded in Galatia, he received "His gospel" by direct revelation from Christ himself (Galatians 1:11). Three years later he went to Jerusalem and got confirmation from Peter and James, the half brother of Jesus, that his revelation was the truth. Paul went on to be named the apostle to the gentiles, with the approval of the Jerusalem church. His letters to the churches he founded make up a big part of Christian doctrine and instruction. So what is the importance of this to the reliability of the NT?

---

70 J. McRay, *Paul: His Life and Teaching* (Grand Rapids, MI, Baker, 2003), 26-27.

Saul/Paul did not see himself as changing religions, as Craig Blomberg writes, "He [Paul] had come to understand that Jesus was the Messiah, a patently Jewish category."[71] And the synagogue leaders accepted Paul as a Jew because he was willing to submit to the synagogue authorities five times receiving the prescribed thirty-nine lashes (2 Corinthians 11:24). So in the case of Paul's life and teachings, he was not following or inventing a new religion, but looking to the fulfillment of the Jewish Messianic hope. As he wrote in Romans 2:28-29, a true Jew was an inward change not an outward sign (e.g. circumcision) and came from God, not men.

Paul presents a problem for liberal scholars of today. They are forced to accept the early dating of his letters, but that confounds their view that belief in Jesus as God was a later evolutionary development by the church. Paul's letters indicate a much more developed Christianity much earlier than they'd like. His letters show a fairly organized church and a developed theology. With the abject failure of liberals to mount a substantial case against the resurrection, the current trend is to attack Paul by claiming he invented a Christian doctrine that was never part of the beliefs of the apostles in the Jerusalem church. Even a superficial read of Acts (by Luke) and Paul's letters shows this to be false. Paul checked in with the apostles on several occasions just to make sure he didn't have a different gospel.

These modern liberal "scholars" collaborated with ABC correspondent Peter Jennings to do the *Jesus and Paul* documentary attempting to show that Paul made up his own religion, which

---

71   C. Blomberg, *From Pentecost to Patmos* (Nashville, TN, B & H Academic, 2006), 89.

would become western Christianity. The only basis for this assertion was the disagreement Paul had with Peter over what requirements of Judaism were still in force (i.e., circumcision and food laws). Peter came to agree with Paul that these were no longer required. Paul and the Jerusalem church affirmed each other's mission. There was never a controversy over the person and work of Christ or what constitutes saving faith. Those controversies came later, well after the text and books of the NT were (for the most part) settled.

Like belief in the resurrected Christ, the conversion of Paul, a Jewish fanatic, can only be explained by some very significant X factor, in this case the encounter with Jesus on the road to Damascus. Theories that his guilt over persecutions or even epilepsy produced his beliefs, beliefs that lasted thirty years of severe hardship, are the stuff of liberal imaginations.

So what do we have? The NT writers were a group of men who knew each other, who were acting on contemporary material from personal experience, and who were writing the same basic story from different viewpoints. The early church, the generation after the apostles, recognized the writings of the apostles. These people never questioned the authorship of the gospels or Paul's major epistles. What can we reasonably conclude about these events? To dismiss early Christian beliefs as just another religious idea would be a show of ignorance. The writings of the NT consist of historically reliable eyewitness testimony of the life and teaching of Jesus of Nazareth, which have been reliably transmitted from two thousand years ago to today with only insignificant differences in the various texts, none of which affect the core beliefs.

The historical evidence stands up well to scrutiny, yet people are deliberately unwilling to thoughtfully consider its implications or instead spend their energies looking for a possible out. An example of this is one friend who dismissed the resurrection of Jesus and the evidence of the empty tomb with the statement, "They haven't found Jimmy Hoffa's body yet either." On one level that is just silly, on another it shows a type of willful ignorance.

A more scholarly example is Jewish NT professor Amy-Jill Levine, from Vanderbilt Divinity School. In an interview she admitted that she basically agrees with all the above evidence in favor of the resurrection, including that the disciples firmly believed they had seen the risen Christ. Yet when asked if *she* believes that Jesus rose from the dead, she replied, "I don't think Jesus' body actually rose from the dead in a physical sense. That so strains *my sense of what is possible.*"[72] [Emphasis added.] Her response is the response of her worldview: scientific Naturalism, with its anti-supernatural bias. No matter how clear the evidence is or its obvious conclusion, she refuses to allow a supernatural explanation.

But will you?

---

72   D. James Kennedy. *Who is This Jesus: Is He Risen?* (Fort Lauderdale, FL, Coral Ridge Ministries, 2002), 90.

Does the Old Testament Support Jesus as Messiah and God?

• • •

In the previous chapter, we examined sound arguments for the historical life and resurrection of Jesus. In explanatory scope and power the statement "God raised Jesus from the dead" far exceeds all naturalistic explanations about the resurrection evidence. Perhaps the most honest rebuttal to the resurrection is to simply say that weird things occasionally happen or seem to occur, and that the resurrection is just one of history's inexplicable events.

C.S. Lewis, when trying to resist the lure of Christianity, wrote "...the hardest boiled of all the Atheists...sat in my room on the other side of the fire and remarked that the evidence for the historicity of the gospels was really surprisingly good."[73]

To help answer the question of whether the resurrection is merely one of the many odd things we can't account for, it is necessary to look at the context of these events. That context is the Hebrew Bible, which Christians know as the Old Testament (OT). The NT is properly viewed as the fulfillment of the OT, especially with respect to Jesus' birth, life, death, and resurrection.

The body of evidence known as Messianic prophecy carries powerful implications for the veracity of the Christian faith. It

---

73 C. S. Lewis, "Surprised By Joy" from the book *The Beloved Works of C.S. Lewis* (New York, Inspirational Press, 1984), 122-123.

affirms the deity of the Messiah (see Isaiah 9:6), a difficult idea for monotheistic Jews, and shows that the God of Israel, the creator of the universe, and the God of both testaments are all one and the same. Christians differ about things like what the creation stories in Genesis are trying to teach and there are at least four major views regarding the book of Revelation concerning the end of the world. With that much up in the air (the beginning and the end!) what does it mean when the Bible claims to be "breathed out" by God (2 Timothy 3:16). To demonstrate this, the Bible has its own internal system of prophecy and fulfillment that makes it self-attesting as to what it actually is, the word of God. If this is the case, then all the other biblical difficulties come down to a matter of interpretation. The key to the predictive nature of prophecy is God's omniscience.

The ability to perceive all of time and space from beginning to end requires a being that exists independent of time and space. The cosmological argument (Chapter 5) concludes that time was created by a personal entity "before" time—this being exists beyond time, and therefore has no beginning, but through it, everything else began. I also argue that the nature of this being is purposeful and intelligent, as well as immensely powerful. If the phenomenon of predictive prophecy in the Bible holds true, this demonstrates that the creator God who sits above time was also involved in inspiring the authors of the Bible concerning future events.

There are many cases in the OT where the prophet makes a prediction that is noted by a later prophet or in one of the historical books. Some of these are controversial. In Isaiah 44:24–45:1, Isaiah, writing in the eighth century BC, named King Cyrus of

Persia who would command the Jewish temple be rebuilt in the sixth century BC. Critics, including some conservatives, find this to be a bit too much and discount the prophecy by saying that there was an ongoing school of Isaiah that continued to write in his name for hundreds of years. The argument is highly technical and turns on the specific details. I can't prove absolutely that the name Cyrus was not added later by someone writing in the tradition of Isaiah after Cyrus was known.

However, I note that it is peculiar that Cyrus, an oriental despot who had conquered the largest empire to date, would consider the Jews to be the chosen people of what he called "the Most High God." First century historian Josephus writes, "I am convinced that he is the God the Israelites worship. He foretold my name through the prophets, and that I was to build his temple in Jerusalem."[74] Cyrus could only know this from reading Isaiah's prophecies given 200 years earlier. I suppose a determined anti-supernaturalist could say Josephus was trying to enhance the prestige of the Hebrew Bible but the fact of the rebuilding of the temple under Cyrus' command is certain history. Josephus was known to shill for his Roman patrons at the end of the first century, but that would give him no reason to make up this sixth century event out of whole cloth.

My next case is free of the "two book theory" surrounding the Isaiah reference to Cyrus. All mainstream scholars I know consider the book of Ezekiel to be a literary unit. Following Judah's deportation to Babylon (586 BC), Ezekiel prophesied the coastal city of Tyre would ultimately be destroyed by a succession

---

74 Paul L. Maier, *Josephus: The Essential Writing (Grand Rapids, MI, Kergel, 1988), 190.*

of nations coming against it. The first would be Babylon under Nebuchadnezzar (Ezekiel 26:3-5). Knowing they couldn't resist Neb's army, the people of Tyre moved to their island fortress one kilometer off the coast.

Eventually, after the time of Ezekiel, Babylon would fall to the Persians (Cyrus), but Tyre would remain unconquered on its island. Hundreds of years later the Persian Empire would fall to Alexander the Great. Alexander used the rubble from destroyed mainland Tyre to build a causeway to the island. All the defenders were killed. And to make sure the city would never regain its status, he had the island scraped bare as it remains to this day.

It would have been one thing for the prophet to predict the destruction of the mainland city, as the Babylonians were already on the march. But for Ezekiel to say that its "...stones and timbers would be pushed into the sea and the island made a bare rock" (Ezekiel 26:12) is miraculous. This didn't happen until after 330 BC, 245 years after Ezekiel wrote and 125 years after the OT was closed to new writing with the last prophet Malachi.

Since we are focusing on the person of Christ, I give this background to show the prophetic tradition was well established by the time Jesus came. His listeners would understand when he said, "The scriptures cannot be broken." So it is important to note that Jesus appealed to prophecy about himself:

- "Then Jesus quoted passages from the writings of Moses and all the prophets, explaining what all the scriptures said about himself." (Luke 24:27)

- "Then he said, 'When I was with you before, I told you everything written about me by Moses and the prophets and in the Psalms must come to be true.'" (Luke 24:44)

Jesus and his followers undoubtedly believed that he was the fulfillment of the OT—the long-promised savior of Israel. The apostle Paul, a rising star in rabbinic Judaism before he became a follower of Jesus on the road to Damascus, went to synagogues to "reason from the scriptures" (the OT) concerning the identity of the Christ (Messiah). Paul certainly knew the scriptures, and many who listened to him were convinced. But one difficulty that Paul faced—and it remains a stumbling block for Jews today— is that a dead Messiah was a failed Messiah. This is not a failure of the scriptures but is rather a reflection of first century Jewish cultural conceptions concerning who the Messiah would be and what he would do. The common expectation was that he would be a deliverer in the archetype of King David and would throw off the Roman oppression. Most of Jesus' Hebrew contemporaries did not understand that the deliverance would be from the shackles of sin, even though this is clearly stated in Isaiah 53.

Before we go further, it is important to note one of the characteristics of Messianic prophecy. This is made clear by the apostle Peter (1 Peter 1:10-12):

This salvation was something the prophets wanted to know more about. They prophesied about this gracious salvation prepared for you, even though they had many questions as to what it all could mean. They wondered what the Spirit of Christ within them was talking about when he told them in advance about Christ's suffering and his great joy afterward. They wondered when and to whom all this would happen. They were told that these things would not happen during their lifetime, but many years later, during yours. And now this Good News has been announced to you by those who have preached it to you in the power of the Holy Spirit sent from heaven. It is all so wonderful that even angels are eagerly watching these things happen.

In other words, the OT prophets that spoke by the Spirit did not fully understand the picture they were painting about Jesus who was to come. Jesus' followers who had witnessed all these things were moved by the spirit to preach them and considered their written word as scripture (2 Peter 1:16-20).

The OT prophets were gradually painting the picture. It is like a boy going to a lake and skipping stones across the surface. Every generation another boy goes to the lake and skips stones from a different angle. A thousand years go by and someone climbs to the top of a tree and sees the words through the water in the lake "God will save his people" and it all becomes clear.

An Address System Concerning Jesus' Identity

By some counts, the OT contains more than three hundred references to the Messiah, *all* of which were fulfilled in Jesus. The following list is not exhaustive, and since I understand that my readers are skeptical, I have purposely eliminated spiritual fulfillments, for example that the Messiah would sit at the right hand of God. That would assume what needs to be proven (Christ's deity), so I will confine my list to those events that arguably occurred in human history and are open to examination. In some ways, the phenomena of prophecy can be thought of as a "miracle in a can." This is because actual or live miracles are dependent on testimony from witnesses. These can be reliable if corroborated and dated as in the NT. However, historical predictive prophecy adds another dimension—it is a written record that remains for us to examine today so we can compare the prophecy with the fulfillment.

Other religions besides Christianity make miraculous claims that are poorly attested by comparison to the NT, and even today there are many who claim to predict the future. But only the NT has predicted miraculous events like the resurrection. In the ancient Hebrew culture, under the law of Moses, the test for a prophet was simple—100% accuracy or death. The Jews took this subject seriously and did not want to fall prey to false prophets. Many prophets made short-term predictions, such as when Jeremiah predicted the Jews would spend seventy years in captivity under the Babylonians. This was a criterion for his writings to be included in scripture.

The Song of Moses—what amounts to Israel's national anthem—foretold the nation's history of disobedience to God, multiple judgments, the shift of God's blessings to others, and the nation's destruction (Deuteronomy 32:1-43). Regardless of some scholar's doubts about its actual date and authorship, think about just how unusual this is. Can you imagine any other nation that has all its negatives laid out in one of its founding documents? Anthems are always used for national exaltation, but Israel's amounts to a lamentation. This should certainly lead us to think that the Bible is a book like no other. This is contrary to *human* nature; we want to think the best of ourselves. This should give more than a hint, given the larger context of the Bible, that it is more than a human production.

The selection process of books for inclusion in the OT was rigorous, and many works that were otherwise good or interesting lacked this divine imprimatur and so were rejected from the Hebrew canon of scripture. However the best was yet to come. Only with the events in the NT could the full outworking of the OT be clearly seen.

The Messianic Strain of the Old Testament

The following list of predictions includes the major Messianic prophecies in the Hebrew canon of scripture, the OT. This list is featured in Josh McDowell's book, *The New Evidence That Demands a Verdict.*[75]

- **He would be born of a virgin.** "Therefore the Lord Himself will give you a sign: Behold, the virgin shall conceive and bear a Son, and shall call his name Immanuel."—Isaiah 7:14

- **He would be called the Son of God.** "I will declare the decree: The Lord has said to Me, 'You are my Son, today I have begotten You.'"—Psalm 2:7

- **He would come from the tribe of Judah.** "The scepter shall not depart from Judah, nor a lawgiver from between his feet, until Shiloh come; and to him shall be the obedience of the people."—Genesis 49:10

---

75   J. McDowell, *The New Evidence That Demands a Verdict.* (Nashville, TN, Thomas Nelson, 1999), chapter 8.

- **He would come from the family line of Jesse, King David's father.** "There shall come forth a Rod from the stem of Jesse, and a Branch shall grow out of his roots."—Isaiah 11:1

- **He would come from the house of David, the son of Jesse.** "'Behold, the days are coming' says the Lord, 'that I will raise to David a Branch of righteousness; a king shall reign and prosper, and execute judgment and righteousness in the land.'" —Jeremiah 23:5

- **His birthplace would be Bethlehem.** "But you, Bethlehem Ephrathah, though you are little among the thousands of Judah, yet out of you shall come forth to Me the One to be ruler in Israel, whose goings forth are from old, from everlasting." —Micah 5:2

Prophecies concerning his nature

- **His preexistence:** "You, Bethlehem, though you are too little to be among the clans of Judah, out of you one will go forth for Me to be ruler of Israel whose goings forth are from old, *from everlasting*."—Micah 5:2 [emphasis added]

- **His being named God:** "For a child will be born to us, a son will be given to us; and the government will rest on his shoulders; and His name will be called Wonderful Counselor, Mighty God, eternal Father, Prince of Peace."—Isaiah 9:6

- **He would fulfill the role of a prophet.** "I will raise up for them a Prophet like me from among your fellow Israelites, and will put My words in his mouth, and he shall speak to them all that I command him."—Deuteronomy 18:18

125

- **He would fulfill the role of a priest.** "The Lord has sworn and will not relent, 'you are a priest forever according to the order of Melchizedek.'"—Psalm 110:4

Prophecies concerning his ministry

- **He would be preceded by a messenger**: "A voice of one crying in the wilderness: 'Prepare the way of the Lord; Make straight in the desert a highway for our God.'" –Isaiah 40:3. **Fulfilled in John the Baptist:** "John the Baptist came preaching in the wilderness of Judea, and saying, 'Repent, for the kingdom of heaven is at hand.'"—Matthew 3:1, 2 (also Mark 1:4, Luke 1:17, John 1:23)

- **His ministry would begin in Galilee.** "But there will be no more gloom for her who was in anguish; in earlier times He treated the land of Zebulun and the land of Naphtali with contempt, but later on He shall make it glorious, by the way of the sea, on the other side of Jordan, Galilee of the Gentiles."—Isaiah 9:1. **Fulfilled:** "Now when He heard that John had been taken into custody, He withdrew into Galilee: and leaving Nazareth, He came and settled in Capernaum, which is by the sea, in the region of Zebulun and Naphtali."—Matthew 4:12-13.

- **He would enter Jerusalem on a donkey**: "Rejoice greatly, O daughter of Zion! Shout in triumph, O daughter of Jerusalem! Behold, your king is coming to you; He is just and endowed with salvation, humble, and mounted on a donkey, even on a colt, the foal of a donkey."—Zechariah 9:9. **Fulfilled on Palm**

Sunday: "And they brought it to Jesus, and they threw their garments on the colt, and put Jesus on it. And as he was going, they were spreading their garments in the road."—Luke 19:35-36. The date of the Messiah's entry into Jerusalem is computed in Daniel 9:24-25, ca. five hundred BC, and fulfilled by Jesus!

Prophecies concerning events after his burial

- **His resurrection:** "For you will not leave my soul in the grave, nor will you allow your Holy One to see decay."—Psalm 16:10

- **He would be betrayed by a friend:** "Even my close friend, in whom I trusted, who ate my bread, has lifted up his heel against me."—Psalm 41:9

- **He would be sold for thirty pieces of silver:** "Then the Lord said to me "Throw it to the potter, that magnificent price at which I was valued by them. So I took the thirty shekels of silver and threw them to the potter in the house of the Lord."—Zechariah 11:13. **Fulfilled:** "What are you willing to give me to deliver Him up to you? And they weighed out to him thirty pieces of silver."—Matthew 26:15. "Then when Judas, who had betrayed Him, saw the He had been condemned, he felt remorse and returned the thirty pieces of silver to the chief priests and elders…But they said 'What is that to us? See to that yourself!' And he threw the pieces of silver into the sanctuary…"—Matthew 27: 3-5

- **He would be forsaken by his disciples.** "Strike the Shepherd that the sheep may be scattered…"—Zechariah 13:7. **Fulfilled:** "And they all left Him and fled."—Mark 14:50

- **He would be silent before his accusers:** "He was oppressed and He was afflicted, yet he did not open His mouth; Like a lamb that is led to slaughter, and like a sheep that is silent before its shearers so He did not open His mouth."—Isaiah 53:7. **Fulfilled:** "And while he was being accused by the chief priests and elders, he answered nothing." –Matthew 27:12

- **He would be wounded and bruised:** "But he was wounded for your transgressions, he was bruised for your iniquities; the chastisement for our peace was upon Him, and by His stripes we are healed."—Isaiah 53:5. **Fulfilled:** "Then he released Barabbas for them; but after having Jesus scourged, he delivered Him to be crucified."—Matthew 27:26

- **He would be crucified with thieves**: "Because he poured out Himself to death, and was numbered with the transgressors…"—Isaiah 53:12. **Fulfilled:** "At that time two robbers were crucified with Him, one on the right and one on the left."—Matthew 27:38

- **His garments would be divided among the executioners, and lots cast for his clothing:** "They divide my garments among them, and for my clothing they cast lots."—Psalm 22:18. **Fulfilled:** "The soldiers therefore, when they had crucified Jesus, took His outer garments and made four parts, a part to every soldier and also the tunic; now the tunic was seamless, woven in one piece. They said therefore to one another, 'Let us not tear it, but cast lots for it, to decide whose it shall be."—John 19:23-24

- **His bones would not be broken**: "He keeps all his bones; not one of them is broken."—Psalm 34:20. **Fulfilled:** " The soldiers therefore came, and broke the legs of the first man, and of the other man who was crucified with Him; but coming to Jesus, when they saw that he was already dead they did not break His legs."—John 19:32-33. *Note:* The Romans would often break the legs of crucifixion victims to hasten death, a practice that had not yet been invented and was therefore completely unknown to the OT writers.

Two other exact fulfillments because of death by crucifixion were:

- **"All my bones are out of joint."** (Psalm 22:14). This is a natural consequence of the crucifixion process, which again was unknown when this prophecy was made.

- **"I can count all my bones. They look and stare at me."** (Psalm 22:17). Because of the extension of the body on the cross, all of Jesus' bones would have been more prominent.

Finally, these exact fulfillments:

- **His side would be pierced:** "So that they will look on Me who they have pierced..."—Zechariah 12:10. **Fulfillment:** "But one of the soldiers pierced His side with a spear..."—John 19:34. *Note:* This was out of character for Roman practice and so therefore it is not likely to be an invention of NT writers.

- **He would be buried in a rich man's tomb:** "His grave was with wicked men, yet he was with a rich man in His death."—Isaiah 53:9. **Fulfilled:** "And when it was evening, there came a rich man from Arimathea, named Joseph... This man went to Pilate and asked for the body of Jesus... And Joseph took the body and wrapped it in a new tomb..."—Matthew 27:57-60

Due to the concentration of material in Isaiah 52:13–53:12, the following has considerable force in favor of Jesus as the Messiah who dies for the sins of his people. For this reason it is often skipped in synagogue readings. This is "The Suffering Servant" passage in full:

> See, my servant will prosper; he will be highly exalted. Many were amazed when they saw him—beaten and bloodied, so disfigured one would scarcely know he was a person. And he will again startle many nations. Kings will stand speechless in his presence. For they will see what they had not previously been told about; they will understand what they had not heard about. Who has believed our message? To whom will the Lord reveal his saving power? My servant grew up in the Lord's presence like a tender green shoot, sprouting from a root in dry and sterile ground. There was nothing beautiful or majestic about his appearance, nothing to attract us to him. He was despised and rejected—a man of sorrows acquainted with bitterest grief. We turned our backs on him and looked the other way when he went by. He was despised, and we did not care.
>
> Yet it was our weaknesses he carried; it was our sorrows that weighed him down. And we thought his troubles were a punishment from God for his own sins! But he was wounded and crushed for our sins. He was beaten that we might have peace. He was whipped, and we were healed! All of us have strayed away like sheep. We have left God's path to follow our own. Yet the Lord laid on him the guilt and sins of us all.
>
> He was oppressed and treated harshly, yet he never said a word. He was led as a lamb to the slaughter. And as a sheep is silent before the shearers, he did not open his mouth. From prison and trial they led him away to his death. But who among the people realized that he was dying for their sins—that he was suffering their punishment? He had done no wrong, and he never deceived anyone. But he was buried like a criminal; he was put in a rich man's grave.

But it was the Lord's good plan to crush him and fill him with grief. Yet when his life is made an offering for sin, he will have a multitude of children, many heirs. He will enjoy a long life, and the Lord's plan will prosper in his hands. When he sees all that is accomplished by his anguish, he will be satisfied. And because of what he has experienced, my righteous servant will make it possible for many to be counted righteous, for he will bear all their sins. I will give him the honors of one who is mighty and great, because he exposed himself to death. He was counted among those who were sinners. He bore the sins of many and interceded for sinners.

What event does this sound like to you?

This passage was instrumental in my conversion to Christianity. Some Jewish rabbis have also turned to Jesus Christ as their Messiah as a result of this passage. However, most rabbis since the Middle Ages argue that the servant is not Jesus of Nazareth, but rather Israel itself. Such a position is untenable—the grammar of the passage points to the servant as a person, not a nation. Also the servant is called sinless, which Israel certainly was not.

Another passage that deserves special mention is Daniel 9:24–27. Though I will not transcribe it here since the Old Testament language regarding dating is obscure to modern readers, there is widespread agreement as to what this dating language means.

After the calculated time period (483 years) from a Persian decree to let the Jews return to Israel, the anointed one will be killed, appearing to have accomplished nothing. Then a ruler [the Roman emperor Vespasian and his son Titus fit perfectly] will raise his armies and will destroy the city [Jerusalem] and the temple.

This occurred in 70 AD. The date in the book of Daniel can be crosschecked with dates in surviving Persian records relating accurately to our modern calendar. The date has the arrival of the anointed one, the Messiah, exactly on Palm Sunday as recorded in the NT. An alternate date held by some scholars still places "the end" by the destruction of the temple in 70 AD.

The date of the book of Daniel has been disputed, with liberals placing it as late as 163 BC, while the traditional date is around 530 BC. But the reference to the Persian decree does not depend on the date of Daniel, as long as the prophecy was written before its AD fulfillment. Not even the most biased scholarship tries to make that case. There are many other elements in this timeline that relate to actual events, but we will not take the time to examine here the elaborate dating structure of the OT and other historical records. The critical point is that the Biblical timeline defies all naturalistic explanations.

Objections to Fulfilled Prophecy

Since it is obvious that many people, notably the Jews, do not believe Jesus is the Messiah, how do modern skeptics attempt to undermine the OT prophecies' validity?

One claim—a potential objection—is that Jesus engineered events to match the OT descriptions. This claim is actually a backhanded compliment to the specificity of OT prophecy. In his popular bestseller, *The Passover Plot*, Jewish NT translator Hugh J. Schonfield proposes that Jesus was an innocent Messianic pretender who attempted to fulfill prophecy in order to substantiate his claims.[76] Schonfield also claims that Jesus was not really dead on

---

76   H. J. Schonfield, *The Passover Plot* (New York, Bantam Books, 1965).

the cross, only drugged (which is absurd). If you look back on the historical Jesus studies (Chapter 8), you will find that Schonfield's idea is similar to the rationale offered by Albert Schweitzer. Rather than belabor this topic with another in-depth analysis, I will simply say that Schonfield's criticisms are unsupported by evidence. Further, there is no possible way that Jesus or any other individual could have controlled all of the necessary events. For example, he would have had no control over where he was born. He could not have controlled his genealogy, which was available at the temple prior to its destruction. The Jews made other arguments against Jesus, but they never questioned his lineage from David, as had been predicted.

Short of being supernatural, there is no way that Jesus could have manipulated the events and people in his life to respond in exactly the way required to fulfill biblical prophecies; this includes the life of John the Baptist, who was born before him. Note that there is no serious challenge to the historicity of Jesus' herald, John.

Another skeptical objection is that the fulfilled prophecies were coincidental, an accident of history. But one statistician has calculated the odds of fulfilling a meager eight prophecies as one chance in 10^{17}. That's roughly the odds of a blind man picking a specific coin out of a pile of coins covering the state of Texas two feet deep. Some still insist on naturalistic explanations for predictive prophecy.

When I was first confronted with passages like Isaiah 53, my initial reaction was to say, "I don't know who wrote this or when." But even if the traditional dates of the OT books are rejected in favor of the later dates of modern criticism, the hard fact is that the entire OT was in place by the third century BC. We know this because the famous library in Alexandria (Egypt) commissioned a translation of the OT, written in Hebrew, into the widely used Greek language of that Mediterranean period. This translation is known as the Septuagint, or LXX. This undeniable fact effectively seals the OT's Messianic prophecies as predictive.

The only charge leveled against predictive prophecy with any legitimacy is that the NT writers took liberties with the OT text. Some skeptics would say the NT's authors ransacked the OT looking for anything that might be applied to Jesus. While this claim is not ultimately valid, I will grant that it has some foundation. First century Jewish interpreters of the OT (this includes the first Christians) came from a worldview with a different conception of history than modern Biblical scholarship. They may have felt entitled to use what they needed without regard for the rules of context used today. Of course, if they really experienced the events of the life of Christ, why shouldn't they be free to use anything in the OT that applied? Regardless, the sheer volume and accuracy of OT material about Jesus overwhelms the charge that the NT writers just picked out the material they found useful.

An example of this kind of interpretation can be found in the infant narrative of Jesus in the gospel of Matthew, where the Holy Family escaping to Egypt to avoid Herod's reign of terror is described. Upon their return, Matthew quotes the OT, "Out of Egypt I called my son." The clear OT sense of this usage is that God was calling Israel (my son) out of Egypt in the book of Exodus.

Matthew felt free to use this typologically as a foreshadowing of the events in the life of Jesus, even though that was not the (only) intent of the original OT author, Hosea. The Bible often works like this. God's action in history leads the first writer to record an event because the spirit of God has moved him to see its importance in redemptive history. Then a second writer looking at another event, in many cases in the life of Christ, sees the greater fulfillment. I see nothing illegitimate in this, especially for the second writer who is living in the fulfillment.

The OT writers were not likely thinking specifically of Jesus. They lived long before Christ and simply wrote about their own circumstances. As King David was scribing the Psalms, thinking in terms of his own life, he managed to come up with what now looks like NT texts complete with details of Jesus' crucifixion. The foreshadowing of King David's Messianic psalms is similar to the foreshadowing in the prophetic books. The Messianic hope of Israel in the Hebrew scriptures was present from Genesis 3:15 forward.

The enormous magnitude of these phenomena across the sweep of the OT comprises a strong supernatural argument that God providentially integrated the lives of OT people and his prophets to foreshadow future NT events.

Was Jesus A False Prophet?

Jesus saw himself as the fulfillment of all three OT offices: king, prophet, and high priest. He was killed in part for claiming to be "king of the Jews," a charge affixed to his cross. A prophet, broadly speaking, speaks for God. Peter (Acts 3:21) saw Jesus as the ultimate future prophet, seen by Moses (Deuteronomy 18:15) as coming from the Jewish people. But the specific test of a prophet was to make a short-term prediction to prove his office and for future inclusion in scripture. Did Jesus ever do that? First he predicted his own death three times, which was good enough for his followers—but only after his resurrection. A dead Messiah was a failed Messiah, so they only fully accepted his prediction *after* the resurrection.

However, Jesus made one astounding prediction that was so improbable that the Jewish leaders and even his own followers couldn't imagine it happening. This was just after he had finished warning the Jewish leadership about the judgment coming upon them for their evil deeds and their rejection of him. Upon leaving the temple (Matthew 24:1-3), his disciples pointed out to him the various temple buildings. He told them, "Do you see all these buildings? I assure you, they will be so completely demolished that not one stone will be left on top of another!" After giving them additional signs of the times to watch for, he answered their question as to when all this would take place. Jesus told them, "I assure you *this generation* will not pass from the scene before all these things take place" (Matthew 24:34). The surrounding context makes it clear he is talking to the people standing before him, not a generation in the distant future.

Confusing Jesus' prophecy to the Jewish leaders with events that are still in *our* future is a common interpretative mistake. The reason for this mistake is because surrounding passages use the language of apocalyptic judgment, and we interpret this "collapsing universe" language as global destruction. For a Jew caught in the siege of Jerusalem, the destruction of the temple *was* the end of their world and happened exactly as Jesus said it would. Severe judgments happened but the world is still here!

We know that this was a real prediction, not something written after the fact, because Luke delivers essentially the same message and we have already seen that Luke/Acts had to have been written prior to the death of Paul under Nero in 66/67 AD. The destruction is in 70 AD. This fulfillment is not recorded in the Bible precisely because the record was already fixed! Matthew's gospel goes to great lengths to point out all the things that were fulfilled by Jesus. If Matthew wrote after the destruction in 70, it is hard to believe he would not be all over the fact that Jesus prediction was fulfilled. So we can be sure from Luke and Matthew that Jesus spoke of these things before they happened!

We can confidently hold that both testaments clearly demonstrate they were overseen by the God of the universe who stands over time.

PART IV

OBJECTIONS TO A
CHRISTIAN VIEW
OF GOD

PHILOSOPHY AND EVIDENCE: THE CATEGORIES OF OBJECTIONS

• • •

There are two principal categories of objections to the Christian faith.

The first category is *philosophical.* Such objections charge that the various doctrines of the Christian faith and the attributes of God (his omnipotence, etc.), are logically incoherent or contradictory. Examples would be the problem of evil and the compatibility of free will with a God that knows the future.

A second category is *evidential.* Since the Christian faith makes claims about certain events that occurred in time and space (i.e., history), a critical question arises: is there enough evidence, on the ground and in the documents, to give weight to these assertions?

On one level, it is important to keep these categories separate; shifting between them can muddle the discussion. Consider the resurrection. We can ask *did it happen* or we can ask *could it happen?* But do you want to be like David Hume and say you shouldn't believe it *even if it did happen* simply because one shouldn't believe in things Hume deems *incredible* (see Chapter 8).

Sometimes this shell game of shifting categories is simply the result of an energetic conversation. But often it is an attempt to evade the implications of good evidence when you don't like where it's leading. It's one thing as a debating tactic; it's another for honest seekers of the truth to mislead themselves as to the real issue. If the evidence supported the truth of the Christian case, would you at least *in principle* be willing to believe it? This often exposes the final type of objection. To say, "I just don't like it" speaks to my earlier point that evidence and worldview can't be separated. In other words, the type of evidence you will commit to is worldview driven.

I've already presented the positive case for the NT. This is a good place to remember that the Christian case is cumulative and although each piece of evidence can be doubted individually, the totality is strong enough to justify forming a belief about the veracity of the Christian worldview. This is similar to the judicial model, where the prosecution presents its evidence and the defense casts doubt on it. As the process continues, the jury may not know what to think until all the evidence is in, at which point a pattern emerges and the evidence demands a verdict. Similarly, in God's economy, you really must choose.

Most folks do not have a well thought out philosophical or evidential objection. They have personal issues. Something about Christianity—or at least what they think is Christianity—doesn't seem right to them. The "new Atheist" movement has put its dislikes on steroids and has sold a lot of books in the process. To put it bluntly, most of their complaints boil down to some form of, "God doesn't run the world the way I would, therefore he doesn't exist." Even when they try to address subjects like the argument from design, it is mostly a rant against the work of the designer. To them, Christianity is not just false, but not worthy of consideration. A negative experience with organized religion, Christian "hypocrites," or negative cultural stereotypes can prejudice the evidence. Jury selection for a trial is a good analogy. Will you consider the evidence impartially? Only in this case it's impossible to get out of jury duty!

In the following sections, I analyze some of the truly intellectual objections to the Christian faith. You will have to examine yourself to see what personal presuppositions and prejudices are keeping you from a fair hearing of the evidence. These answers may not be complete and they may not remove the *emotional* component. I think the answers presented here, at minimum, remove the force of these objections. They can no longer be taken as deal breakers against the Christian case. My minimum goal is to show that Christianity is plausible and worthy of serious consideration.

I can look at critical objections to some of the arguments I have presented and find merit in some of them. There are Atheist thinkers that I admire for their brilliance and intellectual honesty, but these do not include any of the popular Atheists in the media. I know that anyone who rejects the Christian case out of hand is not being serious. The Christian case at least *appears* to be true, and I don't say that about any idea just to show I'm open-minded.

Although I am not a Darwinist, I admit that evolution appears to be true in some sense and certain Christians that dismiss it with simplistic explanations are denying appearances for which we must account. I do reject religions like Islam and Mormonism, along with the belief that the earth is flat, because the problems are glaring and immediate. The case for Christianity cannot so easily be dispensed with; Christianity not only *appears* to be true, but that appearance runs deep—deeper than the arguments for any opposing worldview.

Once the legitimate questions about Christianity are answered, we are forced to face the real underlying issues, which are mostly emotional, social, and based on our desires. A simple question to ask is, "If it were true, would I like it?" The task in becoming a truth seeker is to see past the deceptions and rationalizations we create to maintain a comfortable mental environment, and a comfortable distance from the possibility of a living God to whom we must answer.

Philosophical Objections

If I presented an idea that at first seemed plausible, but you could demonstrate that it violated the laws of logic or involved self-contradiction, then the idea could not be true. Suppose that I said I have a square circle in my pocket. You would not even have to look to know that I have no such object. So, are there any such "defeaters" to Theism in general or to Christianity in particular?

Christianity has a rich philosophical tradition, and most of the objections described here have been answered at some time in the past. However, each generation seems to have to go through the same process. Let's begin with a common example, which is trivial and yet often presented as if it were an ironclad defeater against the concept of God.

Can God make a rock if he cannot lift? If God is omnipotent, then God should be able to make the aforementioned rock. But if God is omnipotent, God should also be able to lift that very same rock. This objection is nothing but linguistic nonsense, like a square circle. God is not required to violate the laws of logic or engage in our language games to establish his omnipotence. The term *omnipotent* does not mean that God can do absolutely anything, such as perform mutually exclusive actions. It simply means God has "all power" to do the possible.

On a more serious note, the great philosopher and mathematician Bertrand Russell offered three defeaters in *Why I Am Not a Christian*[77].

1. **Who made God?** This objection is a version of the question that curious children ask, and many folks who should know better (educated skeptics like Richard Dawkins) still present this as a challenge to Theism. I've dealt extensively with this argument in Chapter 5 in our discussion of the cosmological argument. To recap: An infinite series of causes is logically impossible. Therefore, something (besides a cause-and-effect universe) must be eternal and self-existent, namely God—otherwise nothing at all would exist.

2. **The problem of evil.** Russell's second objection is perhaps the most serious charge that can be leveled at the Christian God, though not necessarily at other gods and religions because they do not make the same claims as Christianity. For example, Eastern Pantheism says that evil is an illusion. This makes sense within a system that grounds everything in

---

77   Bertrand Russell, *Why I am not a Christian and Other Essays: Defects in Christ's Teaching*, (Paul Edward's Edition, 1957), 9.

the impersonal. It has other problems, though. Mainly, most of us just don't believe it to the point of living consistently with this view—we can't help but make moral distinctions. Naturalism/Materialism cannot validly use the terms *good* or *evil* because that would effectively entail ascribing moral properties to some configuration of particles and waves. As such, the problem of evil demands a detailed examination only if one is trying to examine the Christian view of God. I'll address this in more detail shortly.

3. **Jesus promised to return in one generation:** This is Russell's third objection and it falls under the category of evidential rather than philosophical objections. Russell (along with Jews, Muslims, and Atheists) uses this to show that if Jesus couldn't even get his own return right, he is not who he says he is or the text has been corrupted. This is the Muslim view. It is the plain understanding of the apostolic letters that Jesus was to return soon. This clearly happened not as the final judgment in Revelation 20:11-15, but as a coming judgment upon the Jewish system that rejected him. It was the end of the age or the Old Covenant. I have answered this in more detail at the end of the last chapter. I would ask someone like Russell, "Now that I have answered your objections, are you anymore inclined to be a Christian?" That gets to the heart of the issue.

I am not taking lightly what those like Bertrand Russell take as problems or defeaters against the truth of Christianity. But I have found with some digging I usually get a good answer. That doesn't mean I or anyone else has all the answers. Whether it is science, history, the Bible or philosophy, the reasonable man accepts an adequate explanation but the unreasonable man demands proof.

The Problem of Evil

The problem of evil is a serious challenge for the Christian faith. It is difficult to define evil besides "the lack of the good," though philosophers have come up with different categories: moral evil, natural evil (earthquakes, disease, etc.), the imposition of unnecessary suffering on animals, thoughtless degradation of the environment. Regardless of a definition or categories, we all know it when we see it. Some deny it under Evolutionary Materialism or are brainwashed into its denial under pantheistic religious systems. Slogans from the Oprah cohort such as "All is god, god is love, all is love" are mindless and at some level they know it. We are all moral realists when evil gets close enough.

Early in my Christian life, I enthusiastically shared with a friend the evidences I had just learned from reading Lee Strobel's modern classic on the subject, *The Case for Christ*. My friend responded, "Then why did your (expletive) God mess up my (expletive) life. Chronic pain suffered as a result of an ice climbing accident motivated this blast. He followed up with the classic statement—if God exists, there would be no evil—that he learned in a compulsory philosophy class at a Catholic university. He didn't include the rebuttal that an honest professor would have included and I sure didn't know one. Many of the new Atheists wield the PROBLEM OF EVIL like it is a club to bludgeon some well-meaning preacher attempting to answer "Where was your God in _____" (name your tragedy)?

My first response to this attack is to tell the Atheist their use of the word *evil* is illegitimate. Based on their own personal standard, individuals have committed every horror we can imagine. And that's the problem. To define good and evil requires an external standard and that leads to the concept of God. There is no other place big enough to hold this standard. The Eastern/New Age assertion that good and evil are simply appearances to the unenlightened is an unlivable lie. Atheistic humanists try to use a standard of good as what best promotes human flourishing. But that can hardly be decided on. Many of these same ethicists place humans on the same spectrum as animals. Yet it seems obvious that medical experimentation on animals increases our well being at the animal's expense—an obvious contradiction. So of the two alternate worldviews, Pantheism denies evil and Naturalism has no standard to judge it. C. S. Lewis argued the philosophy of Dualism—the world is ruled by good and bad forces—comes about the closest out of all the non-Christian thought systems to solving this problem. But one force or one side can't evaluate the other without reference to a higher standard. Christianity comes close to Dualism, with God, and Satan on opposite sides, but it's not the same. There is no equivalency between God and Satan because God is self-existent and Satan was a free creature created by God who went bad.[78]

Christian apologist and native of India, Ravi Zacharias, put it succinctly in response to the assertion, "There cannot be a God

---

78 C. S Lewis, *Mere Christianity* (New York, Macmillan, 1952), 48.

because there is too much evil in the world" with the following statement:

> When you say there's too much evil in this world you assume there is good. When you assume there is good, you assume there is such a thing as moral law on the basis to differentiate between good and evil. But if you assume a moral law, you posit a moral law giver, but that is who you are trying to disprove and not prove. Because if there is no moral Law Giver, there is no moral law. If there is no moral law there is no good. If there is no good, there is no evil. So what is your question? [79]

One who truly believes in evil must believe in a monotheistic God and later I will argue that only Christianity has a satisfying solution.

The problem stated

1. If God exists, there would be no evil. (This is derived from the "perfect being" concept of God. As to why God must be necessarily perfect, you might want to look up the ontological argument. I have omitted it because it's a two Excedrin headache)

2. Evil exists (by observation).

Therefore: There is no God.

As we have seen before, this is set up as a logical or valid argument. It is also known as the deductive problem of evil. To avoid the conclusion, the Theist must cast doubt on at least one of the premises. Premise two seems to be believed by all but the

---

79   Ravi Zacharias, *Can Man Live Without God?* (Thomas Nelson, 1996), 182.

most indoctrinated of the science of the mind types. Premise one also seems obvious, but is it? A morally good being would prevent all the evil he has the power to prevent, or so it would seem. An omnipresent God (by definition) would have every *opportunity* to prevent all evil so it would seem all evil would be prevented. So premise one seems well supported. But on a closer inspection it isn't. To find out why, we need to see what philosophers do with "a morally good being would prevent all the evil he has the power to prevent." But what if in the process of limiting evil, this being had to forgo a greater good? Doesn't a perfect being have a duty to bring about the greatest good possible? I think most would agree that a world with free creatures capable of love is a higher good than a world of robots programmed to do no harm. But if God is all-powerful, can't he bring about both sets of conditions? Actually he can't and here is why:

1. God cannot do what is actually impossible.
2. It is actually impossible to destroy evil without destroying free choice.
3. But free choice is necessary to a moral universe.
4. Therefore, God cannot destroy evil without destroying this good moral universe.

So the conclusion would be that a moral universe is superior to a non-moral, non-choice universe, as a non-moral universe would lack genuine love. Only if there is the possibility to hate can there be the choice to love.

And you can see that it is impossible for God to do what is self-contradictory. He cannot define a proposition that is both true and false at the same time. Even an all-powerful being cannot make a square circle or a stone that is so heavy he cannot lift it. So even a being that can do anything *possible* cannot make a world with genuinely free creatures with no potential for evil. It is not possible to force people to freely choose the good. Forced freedom is a contradiction. Evil results from and is therefore inextricably linked to free choice. Thus, the only way to destroy evil is to destroy the goodness of free choice. But when there is no moral free choice, there is no possibility of moral good. Therefore, God could not destroy all evil without annihilating free choice as well. God's desire for genuine love outweighs his desire to eradicate evil. So, there are characteristics of the good God that Russell has omitted from his premises, and this is where he fails. He fails to see that a maximally good God would wish to create the maximum amount of good in the world and that entails the risk of free choice and what goes with it.

Alvin Plantinga, perhaps the most noted philosopher of the last forty years, has argued that once free will is given, even an omnipotent God is limited in the possible worlds he can create. Since God must allow for free will in order to create a genuinely moral (good) universe, this entails the possibility—even the necessity—of God's coexisting with evil. The burden is on the Atheist to show otherwise.

However, Christianity holds that even though God could not destroy all evil without destroying all good, nevertheless, he can and will *defeat* all evil without destroying free choice. This argument was summarized by Norm Geisler as follows:

1. God is all good and desires to defeat evil.

2. God is all-powerful and is able to defeat evil.

3. Evil is not yet defeated.

4. Therefore evil will one day be defeated.[80]

Note that the word *defeat* is different from *destroy*. The infinite power and perfection of God guarantees the eventual defeat of evil. Geisler goes on to state:

> The fact that this has not yet been accomplished in no way diminishes the certainty that evil will eventually be defeated. Even though evil cannot be *destroyed* without destroying free choice, nonetheless, it can be *overcome*.

For example, an all-powerful deity could separate the souls of good persons from evil persons according to what those persons freely chose during mortal life. According to Christian theology, those who love God will be separated from those who do not.

A more obvious example of how this might work is as follows I hope most folks reading this find at least some sins, or evil deeds, abhorrent and have no inclination to do them. In the next life people who chose God and are in his presence will find all sin as abhorrent as you find *some* sins now. So even if free will still exists, sin will be unthinkable. So God will have won over evil without taking away free will. This doesn't happen in this world

---

80   N. Geisler, *Baker Encyclopedia of Christian Apologetics* (Grand Rapids, MI, Baker, 1999), 221.

because, while God urges us to choose his way over our own way, this doesn't always happen.

The probabilistic form of the problem of evil

Despite the fact that the deductive form of the problem of evil does not disprove the existence of the Christian God—and I know of no academic philosopher that disagrees with this—the problem of evil still poses a significant problem. While it has just been demonstrated that an all-good God can logically coexist with moral evil, the sheer amount of evil and the types of horrors that we see on earth would seem to make God's existence improbable. This argument is known as the *probabilistic* or *inductive* form of the problem of evil. It cannot be defeated like the deductive form of the argument since there is no specific premise to undercut. It is based on the perception that amount and kind of evil renders God *improbable*.

Moreland and Craig remind us that the crucial assumption behind this reasoning against the existence of God "…is the notion that God cannot have morally sufficient reasons for permitting the amounts and kinds of evil that exist."[81] But is this assumption necessarily true? With all the terrible things in the world, there is still a great deal of good and beauty as well. Despite life's hardships, people generally agree that life is worth living. Even when things are going bad, people characteristically look to the future and hope that things will get better. Now it is possible, given creative freedom (free will), that in any other world of free creatures that is feasible for God

---

81 J. P. Moreland and W. L. Craig, *Philosophical Foundations for a Christian Worldview* (Downers Grove, IL, IVP, 2003), 540.

to create, the balance, hypothetically, between good and evil would be no better than in this world. That is to say, any world containing less evil might also contain less good. Perhaps our world is optimal, containing the most good for the least amount of evil, given free will, the physical laws of the universe, and the constraints of logic.

I remember reading Voltaire's *Candide* in high school. The book was written as a satire against the philosopher Leibniz, who asserted that God did in fact create the best of all possible worlds. As a young cynic, I sided with Voltaire and his list of misfortunes. But one has to keep in mind that God is still restricted by what is logically possible. As finite beings with limited knowledge, we are not in a position to know the calculus of good and evil. I find it interesting that Leibniz was a co-discoverer of calculus. His mathematical mind was likely pondering "possible world" scenarios.

Despite the unlikely aspect of the inductive problem of evil argument, the burden remains on the Atheist to show the amount of evil that would somehow be incompatible with the Christian God. At this point, the argument has become more emotional than philosophical. I do not wish to denigrate the emotional aspect; we have all felt its force. But before shaking our fists at God for allowing suffering, we should consider Atheism: what would a Bertrand Russell say to a child dying of leukemia? "Tough luck, evolution selected you out of the gene pool."

Since I just mentioned sickness, something needs to be said about natural evil or things that happen in nature that cause us harm. God made a real world, not an amusement park. It operates on real physical laws that we must respect because we are creatures and not gods. We don't get to manipulate "the force" no matter what they tell you. Sometimes these laws will harm us under the best of circumstances. The second law of thermodynamics—entropy, or the law of decay—is the most certain law of physics. It brings about the death and decay of everything from protons to the universe. But without it, the biosphere couldn't function and life would be impossible. It is the basis of most disease and our general notion of what is popularly known as Murphy's law (i.e., anything that can go wrong, will go wrong). These laws are a way for God to give us real life experience, to show that this world is broken and to point us to a better one. Despite many good experiences living in the real world, I now, with age and illness, find it somewhat uncomfortable and frightening. But God wants me to stay here a bit longer so I will. I don't know his plan so I have to trust him.

Rather than trusting God, the Atheist feels too much is wrong and if he were in charge things would be different. From this emotional perspective and taking the problem of evil in isolation, the amount of evil seems to count against the *likely* existence of a good God. However, the argument cannot properly be taken in isolation. That is why this section comes after the evidence presented for God. As Craig and Moreland have written, probabilities about personal/historical actions cannot stand alone, but must be considered against relevant background information.

Background Information

Craig argues that relative to the full scope of the evidence, God's existence is probable. If the logical version of the problem of evil were true, then the Christian God would not exist and the case would be closed. But we've already seen that the free will defense defeats the logical or deductive problem of evil argument. However, if the Atheist appeals to the "too much evil" argument and claims that the probabilities are on his side, he can still only hope to win that argument in isolation. But probabilities are relative to one's background information.

To give an illustration, suppose that Joe is a college student. Further, suppose that 90% of college students drink beer. With respect to that information, it is highly probable that Joe drinks beer. But now suppose we find out that Joe is a student at Biola University (a conservative Christian college) and that 90% of Biola students do *not* drink beer. Suddenly, the probabilities of Joe being a beer drinker have changed dramatically. The point is this: probabilities are relative to the background information that one considers.

Background information *is* relevant to the question of God's existence; the arguments we have already examined—cosmological, design, miracles, predictive prophecy, etc.—all have to be taken into account when contemplating the probability of the Christian God. So what you should think about regarding the amount of evil is all the positive evidence for God and the possibility God may have good and sufficient reason to allow a certain amount of evil in our world given the constraints of what *is possible*. Finite creatures certainly don't have all the answers and you should not disqualify God on the way the world seems to you.

Many of the new Atheists use a "divide and conquer" strategy, attempting to undermine Christian arguments one by one. This way they can cast doubt on a specific claim without looking at the whole. This is similar to what a defense attorney does and is momentarily effective against otherwise solid cases, which cause you to doubt all the arguments, one at a time. But in the end, when the jury reviews the case as a whole, the truth becomes apparent.

In just observing the suffering in this world, I would tend to agree that the amount of evil seems to count against the Christian case. But this is the emotional side of the problem of evil. Yet we have shown that God *could* have morally sufficient reasons for making such a world. In fact, despite all its problems, God's creation may be the best of all possible worlds given human moral free will and other logical constraints.

The Atheist looks at the suffering in the world and—overcome with horror, feigned or real—concludes that a good, loving God must not exist. But he still makes moral judgments.

The Pantheist looks at the world's evils and concludes that everything, including evil, is a part of god, or that everything is an illusion. But even the most consistent Pantheist cannot ultimately escape the reality of good and evil: that goodness is right and evil is wrong.

A friend of mine with a ministry to people caught up in alternate spiritualities visited a New Age fair in Denver. One of the presenters, obviously of Jewish decent, had a booth proclaiming, "It is all god." My friend then asked the person in the booth "So tell me, if it is all god, then which part of god was inflicting the horrors of the holocaust on the other part of god?" The person in the booth gave no answer. This shows that the problem of evil has far greater incoherence for worldviews other than Christianity; yet these other views never seem to get the hard question.

The Christian Theist looks at suffering and concludes (from the Bible) that humans have used their moral free will to corrupt the world—to distort life itself from God's original good purpose. Yet only in Christianity is there any hope. To the Christian, God-given free will is not the problem—the problem is the abuse of that freedom, choosing to reject the goodness that God offers in favor of evil. Instead of getting upset at God for giving us freedom—everything is God's fault for not stopping us—the Christian acknowledges that humans are responsible for bringing evil into this world. But this same God that gives us free will sent his own son to be the solution.

So to sum up, philosophy does eliminate at least one form of the problem of evil, the one that would be the end of traditional Theism. Agnostic philosopher Paul Draper concedes: "I do not see how it is possible to construct a convincing argument from evil against Theism."[82] But philosophy can only go so far. My intention here is to break the back of the hardened skeptic's argument. For those who are hurting, I suggest you look to Jesus. Despite the problem of evil, Christianity gives us all hope for a final redemption of all things gone wrong, things that other worldviews dismiss.

No other religion has this. Christianity gives hope, not a dismissal or a mere shoulder shrug. Alvin Plantinga writes:

---

82 William Lane Craig and Chad Meister, *God is Great, God is Good: Why Believing in God is Reasonable and Responsible* (Downers Grove, IL, Inter-Varsity Press, 2009), 108.

As the Christian sees things, God does not stand idly by, coolly observing the suffering of his creatures. He enters into and shares our suffering. He endures the anguish of seeing his son, the second person of the Trinity, consigned to the bitterly cruel and shameful death of the cross....God's capacity for suffering, I believe, is proportional to his greatness; it exceeds our capacity for suffering in the same measure as his capacity for knowledge exceeds ours. Christ was prepared to endure the agonies of hell itself; and God, the Lord of the universe, was prepared to endure the suffering consequent upon his son's humiliation and death. He was prepared to accept this suffering in order to overcome sin, and death, and the evils that afflict our world, and to confer on us a life more glorious than we can imagine. So we don't know why God permits evil; we do know, however, that he was prepared to suffer on our behalf, to accept suffering of which we can form no conception. [83]

Only within the Christian worldview can we find hope in any suffering or evil, for we have a God who understands our suffering. The writer of Hebrews explained to new Christians: "Through the suffering of Jesus, God made him a perfect leader, one fit to bring them into their salvation" (Hebrews 2:10) and "Without wavering, let us hold tightly to the hope we say we have, for God can be trusted to keep his promise" (Hebrews 10:23).

---

83 A. Plantinga, "Self Profile," eds. Alvin Plantinga, James E. Tomberlin, and Peter van Inwagen, (Dordrecht, D. Reidel, 1985), 36.

ADDITIONAL OBJECTIONS

● ● ●

The Hiddenness of God

> They will forsake me and break my covenant...I will forsake them and hide My face from them...Deuteronomy 31:16-17.

While the apparent absence of God is a problem for believers and non-believers alike, Atheists should not take this as evidence that God does not exist. Just as with the problem of evil, God may have perfectly sufficient reason for how much he has revealed and how much he has hidden. This answer may seem annoying, being somewhat recycled from the last chapter, but no one can say it isn't true.

Some say God could solve the hiddenness problem by doing something really dramatic, like Zeus throwing thunderbolts, and that everyone would subsequently believe. But this does not guarantee belief or the kind of belief (trust) that God wants. It seems clear from the Bible that one of the things God wants in his creation are creatures who can freely choose to love or reject him. What sort of world—what state of affairs—would be needed for that freedom?

First, it would need to be a world that would have creatures with the ability to make free moral choices. Second, those creatures would need to exist in conditions where that freedom can be exercised. What sort of conditions might those be? One condition that comes to mind is the absence of pervasive coercion.

Consider the experience of driving a car and noticing a police patrol car in the rearview mirror. You would probably be very careful to stay one mile per hour under the speed limit. Contrast this to the way you drive when you are quite certain that the law is not around. Do you feel a duty to obey the traffic laws because it is the law or due to a motivation of concern for the safety and respect of others?

What if we had the moral police on every corner? Could you freely choose the good with those officers watching? Would you feel free to do the right thing or would that be coercion? At best it would be hard to tell.

The hiddenness objection is also based upon a fundamental fallacy. It assumes that if every human were convinced of God's existence, then every human would freely choose to love God. This is clearly false. The Hebrews, according to their early history, had God living among them. They were reminded of his presence daily through the cloud by day and the pillar of fire by night. But this same early history records their rebellion against him. It's unlikely that human nature has changed much in the intervening years.

Many believers are convinced God has shown himself to be alive and active through his word (scripture) and in their lives. This may be unconvincing to skeptics, but in no case can the apparent absence of God be used as a defeater for his existence, especially by those who have not truly sought him.

But think on this, what if God did do exactly what you asked? What if he showed himself to you to give you a sign? I would wager that many would find some overriding excuse to explain away the miraculous. Tom Morris explains God's hiddenness this way with a thought experiment on whether there is a "snake in my office." He writes,

> Before I look around, I'll presumably lack any sign of a snake. But *before* I look around, I'm in no position to make a negative judgment based on the fact that I don't yet see a snake. *Once* I look around very carefully, and *still* see nothing, I then can deny the claim with good reason.[84]

It's a bit disingenuous to claim there is no God because "I don't see him" when you haven't yet looked for him. What have you done to find him?

Exclusive Truth Claims Are Intolerant

> In the sphere of matters subject to individual thought and decision, pluralism is desirable and tolerable only in those areas that are matters of taste rather than matters of truth.
>
> —Mortimer J. Adler[85]

> "We all pray to the same God."
>
> —Oprah Winfrey,
> speaking at a 9/11 memorial service in New York City.

So who is right? Who in the above quotes do you think may have the authority here? The first is the chairman of the board of editors of the Encyclopedia Britannica and director of the Institute

---

84 T. Morris, *Pascal and the Meaning of Life* (Grand Rapids, MI, Eerdmans, 1992), 95.

85 M. Adler, *Truth in Religion* (New York, McMillan, 1990), 2.

for Philosophical Research; the second is a popular TV talk show host who has been proclaimed as America's "spiritual guide."

In matters of religion, do we choose a pluralistic way of thinking because it is truth, or because of taste? Or as Oprah claims, do we really all pray to the same God?

Religious pluralism is the view that all major ethical religions lead to the same ultimate reality. This fits with ideas like postmodernism, multiculturalism, relativism, and the need for everyone to just get along. To unpack this idea it's necessary to distinguish between various forms of pluralism, especially *metaphysical pluralism* and *social pluralism*.

Democracy in general and in particular the American form that emphasizes individual rights places great value on tolerance, especially in religion. That all religions are tolerated (within some notable limits) or even celebrated does not mean they are equally true. I call this *naive pluralism*, as a little reflection will show. It is not much more than political correctness. The acceptance of this form of social pluralism does not imply the truth of metaphysical pluralism—that all religions point to the same ultimate reality.

Despite some superficial similarities in ethics, the world's religions have vastly different ideas about God's properties (impersonal, personal, super personal), creation, sin, salvation, time (linear or cyclical), God's relationship to the world (in it, out of it, or both), and what happens when you die.

It is this last item, the afterlife, which has the most significance because it happens to *you* and it is *forever.* As I stated in the introduction, and this is beyond dispute, *something* happens when you die, and the outcomes are mutually exclusive. Anyone who fails to acknowledge this is either not acquainted with what the world's religions really teach or is affirming *different* realities at the same time. This is what is meant by metaphysical pluralism. It is obviously false on this ground that all religions say the same thing.

A somewhat more sophisticated form of pluralism is *epistemic pluralism*. It refers to our inability to know truth exhaustively. As an appeal to humility, this may be good. But when taken as an absolute it can lead a person into contradictory beliefs. Leading Pluralist thinkers like John Hick claim that the contradictions among the world's religions are only apparent, not real. Perhaps all religions experience the same divine reality in different ways. Douglas Geivett analyzed Hick's position and wrote, "[according to Hick] All of the great religious traditions of the world represent authentic responses to transcendent reality, and yet none of the descriptions of the Transcendent embodied in the various traditions…is *literally* true."[86]

Hick popularized the "elephant analogy" to explain differing religions. In this word picture, several blind men examine an elephant and each concludes the part he touches represents the whole, while missing the big picture. Hick appeals to Kant's philosophy that we can't know the thing in itself, we only know the world of appearances and in the case of ultimate being, or in Hick's words, "the real," it is mediated through different religions. So the examples of leaders such as Jesus, Muhammad, the Buddha, and Krishna are only revealing one part of a greater whole. Hick

---

86 R. D. Geivett, *Evil and the Evidence for God: The Challenge of John Hick's Theodicy.* (Philadelphia, Temple University Press, 1993), 38.

places a supra-religious category over all religions to create harmony where none is apparent.

Other proponents of this view, like Joseph Campbell, speak of god (small g) as an "ineffable (inexpressible) ground of being."[87] Of course Campbell just spoke something about God that he believes is true. During his interview with Bill Moyers, he plainly states that all the great religions, such as Christianity, Buddhism, and Islam, are religions that all teach the same thing. Campbell speaks of religious claims (myths) as metaphorically true but literally false. With this teaching Campbell, like Hick, has just placed himself above all religions. He has in effect declared them all false and only he knows the truth. It seems that he is setting out to be a new mythmaker in order to enlighten the benighted. This is the most arrogant of all positions when you consider both Hick and Campbell are proponents of belief in only their religious ideas, which are to deny all other religious beliefs.

Holding to religious pluralism is internally self-refuting. The great religions of the world are *not* the same, nor can they be forced into harmony. If Hinduism features an impersonal force, Buddhism is at its heart atheistic, Islam's Allah is totally transcendent and impersonal, and Christianity has a personal savior in Jesus Christ; it is irrational to think these can be united. It is obvious that Hick and Campbell's ideas of pluralism are self-refuting. God cannot be both knowable and unknowable, both personal and impersonal.[88]

---

87 Joseph Campbell and the Power of Myth with Bill Moyers (PBS, 1988).

88 For another concise explanation, see the booklet by Doug Groothuis, *Are All Religions One?* (Downers Grove, IL, IVP, 1996).

St. Paul, certainly an exclusivist, held to the claim of the resurrection based on his own eyewitness testimony and the reports of others (1 Corinthians 15). But he said "…If Christ has not been raised, your faith is worthless…If we have hoped in Christ in this life only, we are of all men most to be pitied." (1 Corinthians. 15:17, 19) This notes an interesting point about Christianity: that it is testable. No other religion can truly be examined, because the religious experience is going on inside a person and is therefore not truly testable. But St. Paul realizes that being wrong, despite the solid foundation for his beliefs, entails negative consequences. Pluralists, however, press their assertions that all religions are true, based on their own say-so, without even the slightest appeal to evidence!

Curiously, it is the very appeal to evidence that so offends the religious pluralist. Craig Hazen related a story of witnessing Christian apologist John Warwick Montgomery, a scholar and lawyer, who advocates an evidential/historical approach to Christian truth claims. Addressing a symposium on world religions, Dr. Montgomery's paper was written as a dialogue between Sherlock Holmes and Dr. Watson. In it, Holmes was working through important questions of all religions using the logical and factual approaches that made the character famous. As related by Hazen, some in the audience became visibly disturbed.

The moment the lecture was over; one professor jumped up and blurted out, "Dr. Montgomery, you do tremendous harm to religion!" What sort of damage did he do? As Craig Hazen writes:

> Like matter and antimatter, faith and fact cannot come into real contact without destroying something. Indeed, the reason faith and fact are

usually kept in separate, hermetically sealed compartments… First, it is postulated that, *a la* Immanuel Kant, fact and faith simply have no point of interaction by definition—to force them to deal with one another is simply a category mistake. Second…it is fundamentally *immoral* to allow such interaction because it undermines the sacrosanct agenda of religious pluralism[89]

In Hazen's analysis, Montgomery had subjected religious questions and claims to methodologies available to us all. In his estimation, if the tools and methods of the scientist, historian, philosopher, and lawyer could be brought to bear on the truth claims of various world religions, then, in Hazen's words, "…the very ethos of an entire discipline would implode."[90]

Christian apologists are willing to risk this kind of inquiry because they are confident their worldview can withstand the scrutiny. The Christian case has some loose ends that are not (yet) settled to everyone's satisfaction, but in comparison, the rest of the world's religions do not even try to make a case for correspondence to the real world, at least on any objective basis. Academics committed to religious pluralism hope to save their discipline (and possibly their jobs) by removing the object of their study from any connection to the real world. All they have left is the study of how people *feel* about religion. A university's department of religion may be little more than a thinly disguised branch of the anthropology department.

---

89   C. Hazen "Ever Hearing but Never Understanding" in *Tough-Minded Christianity*. Eds. W. Dembski and T. Schirrmacher (Nashville, TN, B & H Academics, 2008), 21.

90   Ibid., 21.

So who set the rules for religious studies? The root of this question again comes out of the thinking of Enlightenment philosopher Immanuel Kant (ca, seventeenth century). According to Kant, facts and faith simply have no point of contact by *definition*.[91]

Today's religious academy has used Kant's assertion because to allow for such contact (between the believer and the object of his or her belief) undermines the whole agenda of modern religious studies. Montgomery's ideas of testing religious claims are considered dangerous because it puts some beliefs in jeopardy. Faith is held to be an irrational and untestable proposition, so John Montgomery's Sherlock Holmes was snooping around in areas that were morally off-limits to the rulebook of pluralistic ideology.

I hope you can see that pluralism is the worst of all possible positions with respect to religious truth. Pluralism denigrates the truth claims of all religions without offering anything to commend itself besides skepticism and political correctness. At least Atheism makes a specific claim based on a perceived lack of evidence or logical incoherence. All three Western monotheisms (Judaism, Christianity, and Islam) at least in their traditional forms, make mutually exclusive truth claims, especially with respect to the deity of Christ. And the claims made by Hinduism and Buddhism are in contradiction to the Western monotheisms. Finally, it is inconsistent for there to be any truth in a pluralistic view of

---

91 Kant claimed that to conflate the two would be a category mistake. This is based on the assertion that to see the reality behind faith is impossible because there is a wall between them. For Kant to know this, he must be able to see behind his own wall! For additional reading see F. Schaeffer, *The God Who is There* (Downers Grove, IL, IVP, 1998).

religions, for when you compare all the world's great religions, each makes specific claims regarding truth that are in contradiction to each other. They simply cannot be harmonized. As with Hick, attempts to harmonize their claims, instead discards them and replaces them with entirely different claims.

While you should be convinced that metaphysical pluralism (all religions point to the same ultimate reality) is untenable, you are probably still resisting the exclusivist claims of Christianity. One reason for this is that simple observation shows that many non-Christians seem to be leading better lives than many Christians. So how can a Christian claim to be "saved" while the righteous Pagan is "lost"? This misconstrues the very nature of the Christian claim that all men are sinners and cannot pay their own debt to God. It also presumes a human standard for what is good, and gives you the god-like ability to read the thoughts and intentions of a human heart.

When Jesus was asked about the greatest commandment, his answer was in two parts. He said, "You shall love the Lord your God with all your heart, and with all your soul, and with all your mind...You shall love your neighbor as yourself" (Matthew 22:37, 39). Even with a good try at "loving your neighbor," the willful neglect of loving God with the entirety of your being (heart, soul, and mind) leaves you short. Fortunately, God has a nonexclusive plan available to all, and free for the asking.

Those who wish to base their salvation on human effort, the position of non-Christian religions, both Eastern and Western, have another problem—how much effort is enough? The question of "saved" or "lost" cannot be put on a continuum. It's like being pregnant—you either are or you're not. So some binary event like a decision to trust in Christ makes more sense than a sliding scale of good vs. bad deeds. Islam works by weighing one's goods against the bad, with a good measure of capriciousness by Allah thrown in. Islam's followers never have assurance of how they have been weighed in the balance and what their final outcome will be, except in the case of jihad or martyrdom. This has lead to some tragic behaviors.

Since the United States is, for the most part, a meritocracy, it seems only natural to our culture that one must earn salvation. Merit may be good in principle in many organizations but it is a poor basis for love, whether between parents and their children or between God and his children. In fact merit or performance is the way of the world and the world's religions follow the world's pattern. It is the free lunch of Christianity's offer of God's grace (un-merited favor) that does not conform to the pattern of the world. This is another reason to believe that Christianity is not a man-made religion.

Jesus claimed the he was the only way to be reconciled to God (John 14:6). This statement is as divisive today as when he made it. It is doubtful God would have validated that claim by raising Jesus from the dead had it not been true. Christianity has knowable truth rather than creative myth. But truth by its very nature is exclusive and should be welcomed by all thinking people. Truth in religion should be at least as valuable as truth in any other aspect of existence.

The Universe Is Too Big

This may seem like an odd statement, but it comes up a lot. I have a good friend, a retired astronomer, who states, "The universe is just too big!" In his mind God cannot exist because of the size of the universe, and he has been discussing this issue with me for years. I think he believes I fail to grasp the size of the argument! Those who hold this view look at the apparent immensity of the universe and cannot conceive of any reason God would make it so big compared to us. This is in essence the "wasted space" argument. Carl Sagan used it on his *Cosmos* series. It is also an "I would not have done it that way" argument that underlies most of the objections that Atheists present.

This can be answered three ways: philosophically, theologically and scientifically.

Philosophically, this is what is known as a category mistake. Why should a spiritual entity conform to a physical standard? What does the size of the universe mean to a spirit?

Theologically, the Christian God is both infinite and personal. What does the characteristic of personality have to do with size of the universe? Would we be more important to God if the earth and we were larger in relation to the rest of the universe? At one time Enlightenment thinkers following Kant had the expectation that an infinite God would require an infinite universe. Learning that the universe was finite would have been construed as a theological problem. This then is a pseudo-dilemma dependant on your philosophical leaning.

Scientifically, the size/mass of the universe is by necessity. Once God decided the initial laws, everything else necessarily followed. Let me explain.

171

Assuming a universe that is intelligible, all that we see must be *necessary* according to the laws that were there at the beginning. God presumably could have made another possible world, but he had to pick *some* world (universe). Once he chose this world from all possible worlds he could have created, he would be committed to following its logic, his own logic, as to how the world unfolds.

Life—any life—requires carbon for complexity, because complexity is the hallmark of life. Carbon requires a certain physics, which requires certain initial conditions at the start of the universe. Those conditions, which include its mass, expansion energy, and a whole bunch of other exotic stuff, were built into the big bang, which was ironically much, much smaller than us when it started. (No one argues that the universe is too small!)

Those initial conditions evolved or unfolded by necessity into a universe that would permit life. Complex life is only possible in a universe this old and therefore this size. As our universe expands, life will again become impossible in the future when the universe really does become too big and suffers its inevitable heat death. However, that is so far in the future that it does not affect our discussion here.

Could God have done it differently? I suppose so, but not once he chose the initial conditions, and not if he wanted to be consistent so that we could see that the universe is intelligible and know there is a mind behind it all. The Bible says that God makes his existence plain through his creation. St. Paul writes in Romans 1:20, "For since the creation of the world His invisible attributes, His eternal power and divine nature, have been clearly seen, being understood through what has been made…"

THE BIBLE: HARD TO BELIEVE?

● ● ●

The Bible, a collection of about sixty books depending on how they are divided up, was written over a period of fifteen hundred years in locations from Egypt to modern Iraq and Turkey. It contains a variety of literary genre: historical, legal, prophetic, and apocalyptic, as well as the wisdom literature and poetic forms used in worship. As we saw in Chapter 10, there is a predictive element found in most of biblical literature (not just in the books written by the prophets) that seals the fact that the contents are beyond human authorship. With that as a firm foundation for trust in the "God breathed" or inspired nature of scripture (2 Timothy 3:16), I admit to many puzzlements and unanswered questions. This is to be expected by the very nature of the material, which was written long ago and far away, and which consists of a rich variety of literary types that are unfamiliar to the modern mind. This is especially true of the apocalyptic genre, including some of Daniel, Ezekiel and most of Revelation. These books contain symbolic unveilings of things to come.

The new Atheists—Dawkins, Hitchens, *et al*—do their utmost to use the strangeness of the OT to rage against God. They do this with little attempt to understand the cultural backdrop and immediately judge its strangeness by their own culturally conditioned standards.

Issues about proportional punishment (eye for an eye), dietary laws, slavery, alleged genocide and general weirdness seem to make the God of the OT irrelevant or incomprehensible to the modern mind. Even for Christians, the God of the OT seems far removed from the Jesus portrayed in the NT. OT scholars have investigated these issues for some time, but their work is difficult to understand for those outside the discipline. If you are honestly bothered by God's actions in the OT, there is an excellent book on the subject by Paul Copan (*Is God a Moral Monster?*), which answers many of these questions. [92]

Even within conservative Christianity, scholarly debates continue over the nature of God's revelation in scripture. It would be a mistake for someone deciding whether to put their faith in Christ to place much weight on the details of this debate. Your focus should be on the identity of Jesus and his resurrection. When the Bible clearly claims to be giving a historical narrative, it has been found accurate at its points of contact with secular history. On disputed historical questions, the Bible has time and again been proven correct, often against prevailing scholarly wisdom.

Archeology and the Bible

When I was first looking into the reliability of the Bible, especially the OT, the conservative scholars I was reading said that the Bible was well supported by archeology. A friend who knew of my enthusiasm for my new faith sent me a *Harper's* article that claimed new findings showed the early stories about Israel were essentially a

---

92 P. Copan, *Is God a Moral Monster? Making Sense of the Old Testament God* (Grand Rapids, MI, Baker, 2011).

pious fraud with no evidence they were stories made up at a much later date to provide a national identity. I was troubled and so were thousands of Christians who were calling on their pastors for an explanation. After obtaining a subscription to *Biblical Archeology Review* (BAR), I was shocked to find how little consensus there was about certain key events, such as the date of the Israelite conquest of Canaan and it implication for things like the battle of Jericho.

In archaeology, like most everything else, facts need interpretation. Still, it is undeniable that there are many points of contact between what's found in the ground and the biblical record. So why do Jewish and non-conservative archeologists protest what they see as fundamentalists usurping the proper use of their discipline to prove their religious claims? But here's the thing: the same archeologists who write angrily about the misuse of their trade to support biblical religion continue to maintain that their findings confirm, for the most part, that the Bible is generally reliable. [Note: I later found that the *Harper's* article cites the work of a school called Biblical minimalism and is not reflective of any kind of consensus.]

According to Menahem Mansoor, a professor emeritus at the University of Wisconsin at Madison:

> Biblical archeology's greatest significance is that it has corroborated many historical records in the Bible. Biblical archeology has failed to deter people who seek to validate religious concepts by archeological finds. These people should not confuse fact with faith, history with tradition, or science with religion.[93]

---

93 Menahem Mansoor, "Scholars Speak Out," *Biblical Archeology Review*, (June 1995), 29.

Israel Finkelstein, professor of archeology at Tel Aviv University says:

> The most obvious failure of Biblical archeology has been the use of old biblical archeology by semi-amateur archeologists...These were times of desperate attempts to prove the Bible was correct.[94]

Also from Tel Aviv University, David Ussishkin states:

> A fundamental question asked by all the world in the last two centuries is, Is the Bible true? Do the narratives related in it represent real events and are the figures mentioned real people who lived and acted as the biblical text tells us they did?...In general the evidence of the material culture fits the biblical account beginning with the settlement of tribes of Israel and the land of Canaan and the establishment of the Kingdom of Israel. Hence, archeological data are consistent with the view that at least this part of the biblical account is in general, historically based.[95]

So here we have eminent scholars admit that the evidence demonstrates that the historical record is generally reliable. Yet they warn us not to draw religious conclusions when the very book they are describing as accurate tells us to do just that! Christian apologist Greg Koukl asks, why not? Because (say the scholars), this would be confusing history with religion and facts with faith. This is the same class of objections we saw with the argument from design. But this is exactly the feature of Judaism, and by extension Christianity, that make its claims that God acted in history viable, that its religious claims are rooted in history, that

---

94 Israel Finkelstein, "Scholars Speak Out," *Biblical Archeology Review*, (June 1995), 27.

95 David Ussiskin, "Scholars Speak Out," *Biblical Archeology Review*, (June 1995), 32.

God acts in and through history. When God acts this way, he leaves his fingerprints on history in an objective way that can be looked at and analyzed today.

So when academic archeologists acknowledge that their research largely supports the Bible and in their next breath say this doesn't mean the Bible is true, what are they doing? They are doing what modern man must do to be, well, modern: maintain the fact/faith distinction. This keeps modern man safe from the tyranny of a true religion but it comes at great cost.

Dr. Francis Schaeffer explains that this is the malady of modern man. In several of his writings Schaeffer gives us a picture of a two-story house with no stairway connecting the upper story with the lower. The lower story consists of one kind of reality: the laws of science, rationality, logic or as some would say, the world as it is. The upper story is where values, meaning, religion, and God, such as we make of him, dwell. According to Schaeffer, this is the tragedy of modern thinking. We can't bring the two stories together. When this happens, says Schaeffer, an individual or an entire culture drops beneath a line of despair. There is no way for religion, morality, or any of the higher values to be extracted from the details of the world, including the Bible. So just as the methodological Naturalists, many of them "religious," forbid the use of science as a pointer to God, likewise the biblical archeologists become angered whenever anyone tries to use their discoveries to demonstrate what God has revealed to man. The same can be said for the use of predictive prophecy. If a person wants these things, one must make the existential leap of faith and unplug from the real world. Unfortunately, many seminaries and theologians are stuck in the upper story. What they serve up isn't truth and the folks know it. It has gutted traditional faith of its power.

It Is His Story

Throughout the span of the Bible, there is a unifying theme of God's creation, man's fall into sin, and God's plan of redemption. Another way to put the Bible's story is: God made us, we blew it, Jesus paid the price; you need to accept his gift. This unifying theme, written without many of the writers being aware of the others' work, is further evidence of its inspiration. Inspiration is what the Bible claims about itself: "All scripture is God breathed."

What does this actually mean? It does not mean that God dictated it, except when the Bible explicitly states that is the case, as when a prophet says, "Thus says the Lord." Even then we can tell that God is working through human agency, preserving the character of the writer. Christian fundamentalists often err on the side of seeing only the divine nature of the Bible while liberals and the unbelieving, noting the obviously human character of the work, are blind to its inspiration. A balanced view is to acknowledge both: The superintendence of God working through human personalities.

Another misconception is that modern Christians are picking out the parts we want to believe. If we were more consistent we would still be stoning adulterers. One history professor said I failed to follow the Bible because I ate shrimp, which is contrary to the law of Moses! The principle here is that new revelation trumps old revelation. Christ himself ended the civil and ceremonial laws of Israel, saying through him they were fulfilled. The theocracy of Israel was a temporary measure until "...the right time..." (Galatians 4:4). God brought his son into the world as his final revelation.

The NT or new covenant is about the life of Christ. Most of the attention is given to his three-year ministry with the focus on the week before his crucifixion. I have already given extensive evidence for believing in the reliability of these accounts. God showing up in person is a logical place to end the story. What more could be revealed? Jesus is the "very image of the invisible God" (Colossians 1:15). What his followers wrote after his death and resurrection is a careful history of the first thirty years of the early church, letters of instruction from the apostles, and a prophetic/apocalyptic book about the end of the old covenant and the final judgment (Revelation).

The book of Revelation is obviously meant as a book end to the Bible. It was likely written by John, the last apostle and the only one to avoid martyrdom and witness what Jesus called "the end of the age," (the end of the old covenant) with the destruction of the Jewish temple.

There is no reason to consider any of the spurious books written 100-200 years after the apostles (the Gnostic gospels) as part of the Biblical canon. There is no apostolic witness to these books and they are of a fanciful nature that's opposite to the plain reporting in the gospels. When you consider other candidates for new revelation that came after the Bible—like the Koran or the Book of Mormon—they lack any corroboration by witnessed miracles.

They are claims without support. I can't emphasize this enough. There is a vast difference between a book from a single author that claims to be a revelation from God and a collection of books by a variety of authors attesting to the same events and miracles and which contains an internally consistent message. Whether you believe the miracles or not, you simply can't compare the veracity of the two types of evidence. There is good reason for the multiple authorship of the Bible. The Bible itself calls for a judicial standard: multiple witnesses. The *Koran*, the *Book of Mormon*, and others like that of the Baha'i faith utterly fail this standard.

With the proper interpretive skills (or a good study Bible with commentary) the Bible should not be hard to believe provided one is not committed to philosophical Naturalism. One must also not judge the book by modern historiography. This is not video cam reporting. One must also not resort to other forms of chronological snobbery such as when ancient standards of behavior don't comport with how you think the people in the Bible should have acted and how God acted. Many reject the Bible because some aspect just rubs you wrong. The Bible is a book about God's action in the world and it does contain prophecy and miracles. If one's worldview finds all this incredible, you might do well to remember Naturalism fails to answer the big questions of creation, design, purpose and the difference between good and evil, except as a matter of preference. If God exists, we shouldn't be surprised that he reveals himself to his creatures. The Bible towers above all other candidates for such a revelation.

GOD'S GRACE AND SALVATION

• • •

T he Bible teaches that it is impossible for humans to enter the kingdom of heaven, in this life or the next, through their own efforts. Jesus' own clear teaching and that of his followers is that we must accept him as our lord and savior in order to be saved from the consequences of our rebellion against God. This is what separates Christianity from other world religions, many of which share similar ethical principles. Forgiveness by God, through Christ alone, without the need to earn it by doing good works, is both Christianity's greatest strength and, for many, its biggest stumbling block. It is a bigger problem for many today than the existence of miracles, which many spiritual people accept in some form.

Popular Atheist Christopher Hitchens, author of *God is Not Great*, made the charge that Christianity at its core is hypocritical. He stated that on the one hand God tells his followers, "...you are contemptible and worm like...but the whole universe was designed with you in mind!" This is a huge misappropriation of the doctrine of "original sin" coupled with the fine-tuning argument.[96] Hitchens is also known for saying that Christianity's salvation by

---

96 From the Craig/Hitchens debate 2010.

grace doctrine has to be completely immoral, since it implies that people can avoid responsibility for their sins by letting Jesus take the fall. For Hitchens to sit in judgment on what is moral is a farce under his Materialist ethic.

Non-Christian religions make similar charges. Mormons often argue that "salvation by grace" is nothing but a James Bond 007 "license to sin"; hence the Church of Latter Day Saints teaches a "salvation by works" system (you have to do enough religious works to earn your way to heaven). Islam has a list of obligations but in the end it is purely a matter of Allah's will—one never knows for certain unless one dies in jihad.

According to C.S. Lewis, the *distinguishing* feature of the Christian faith is salvation by grace (God's unearned favor). Pastor Tim Keller of Manhattan's Redeemer Presbyterian Church has been very successful in reaching anti-religious twenty- somethings with the message of grace, which he explains as follows:

> There is...a great gulf between the understanding that God accepts us because of our efforts and the understanding that God accepts us because of what Jesus has done. Religion operates on the principle "I obey—therefore I am accepted by God." But the operating principle of the gospel is "I am accepted by God through what Christ has done—therefore I obey."[97]

Tim Keller continues by pointing out the difference in "religion" versus the gospel, or the "good news." The fundamental difference is between a fear-based system trying to meet God's standards in order

---

97 T. Keller, *The Reason for God: Belief in an Age of Skepticism* (New York, Riverhead Books, 2008), 186.

to keep one's blessings compared with a motivation of gratitude over a finished work by Jesus Christ. The difference, Keller points out, is "…The moralist is forced into obedience, motivated by fear of rejection; a Christian rushes into obedience, motivated by a desire to please and resemble the one who gave his life for us."[98]

In his explanation, Dr. Keller emphasizes the distinction between mere religious obligation, and surrendering to what he terms the "threat of grace":

> When many first hear the distinction between religion and the gospel they think that it sounds too easy. I know I thought, "This is a really good deal." If that is Christianity, all I have to do is get a personal relationship with God and I can do anything I want. Those words however can only be spoken from outside the experience of radical grace. No one on the inside speaks that way. In fact, grace can be quite threatening.[99]

Dr. Keller goes on to tell of meeting a woman who had gone to church growing up and yet had never heard the distinction between religion, rules and ritual, and the gospel—the good news that Jesus has made us acceptable to God. She had always heard that God will only accept us if we are good enough. She explained to Keller:

> If good works saved me there would be a limit to what God could ask of me or put me through. I would be like a taxpayer with "rights"—I would have done my duty and now I would deserve a certain quality of life. But if I am a sinner saved by sheer grace—then there's nothing he cannot ask of me.[100]

---

98 Ibid., 87.

99 Ibid., 1, 89.

100 Ibid., 189.

At the heart of her statement is the realization that true salvation requires a savior. To accept this gift, you need to understand what Jesus has really done. He has paid in his own humanity and divinity the penalty for your freedom. So in accepting this costly grace, gaining your freedom, you joyfully want to give back something to show your love and gratitude. But once you understand the size of the gift given and the cost to God himself, to accept the gift is to allow him to change you, not the other way around.

All other faith commitments and religions ask their followers to learn from a certain set of teachers a way to salvation. Keller writes:

> The founders of every other major religion essentially came as teachers, not as saviors. They came to say, "Do this and you will find the divine." But Jesus came essentially as a Savior rather than a teacher... Jesus says: "I am the divine come to *you*, to do what you could not do for yourselves."[101]

From the inside of grace, the motivation is all joy. Reformed slave runner John Newcomb captured this in his famous hymn, *Amazing Grace*:

> 'Twas grace that taught my heart to fear
> And grace my fears relieved.
> How precious did that grace appear the hour I first believed.

This may seem the greatest paradox of all. The most liberating act of free, unconditional grace demands that the recipient desire to live their life according to the one who is the giver—the one who gave his life for you.

---

101 Ibid., 192.

This final note from the writings of Tim Keller is a reminder to help explain what happened in the substitutionary death of Jesus, and by substitutionary I mean this: God himself took on the ultimate suffering and took the sins of the whole world upon himself. Remember this:

> It is crucial at this point to remember that the Christian faith has always understood that Jesus Christ is God. God did not... inflict pain on someone else, but rather on the Cross absorbed the pain, violence, and evil of the world into himself. Therefore the God of the Bible is not like the primitive deities who demanded our blood for their wrath to be appeased. Rather, this is a God who becomes human and offers his own lifeblood in order to honor moral justice and merciful love so that one day he can destroy all evil without destroying us.[102]

That God would want to reach out to us so badly that he would become a real human being and take on himself the penalty that we deserved is the miracle and mystery of true love and forgiveness.

But I'm Spiritual, So Why Do I Need God?

C. S. Lewis spoke of a phenomenon in England forty years ago of what he called "Life-Force philosophy." Lewis expounds:

> When people say this, we must ask whether they think this has a mind or not. If they do, then a "mind bringing life into existence and leading it to perfection" is really God, and their view is thus identical with the Religious. If they do not, then what is the sense that something without a mind "strives" or has "purpose"? This seems to me fatal to their view. One reason why many people find

---

102 Ibid., 200.

Creative Evolution so attractive is that it gives one much of the emotional comfort of believing in God and none of the less pleasant consequences. When you are feeling fit and the sun is shining and you do not want to believe the whole universe is a mere mechanical dance of atoms, it's nice to be able to think of this great mysterious Force rolling on through the centuries carrying you on its crest. If, on the other hand, you want to do something rather shabby, the Life Force, being a blind force, with no morals and no mind, will never interfere with you like that troublesome God we learned about when we were children. The Life-Force is a sort of tame God. You can switch it on when you want, but it will not bother you. All the thrills of religion and none of the cost. Is the Life-Force the greatest achievement of wishful thinking the world has yet seen?[103]

This pantheistic spirituality continues to gain ground, it appeals to our vanity to be told to look for the god within. The Life-Force is not open to verification or falsification, unlike the historical Jesus, and it does not matter if you believe in it or not. It offers limited psychological benefits in this world and offers, like Atheism, nothing for a world to come. How is dissolution of the soul (ego) into spiritual nothingness any better than decaying into dust? At bottom, Life-Force spirituality, Pantheism and Eastern Religion are nothing but spiritualized Naturalism. Are you really okay with this outcome? Many of you have told me you are. I would hope that you would hope for something better.

If we are to competently examine the question of eternity—including Theism in general and Christianity in particular—we must not get stuck in the halfway house of "spirituality." I am

---

103 C. S. Lewis, *Mere Christianity* (San Francisco, HarperCollins, 1952), 26-27.

confident that there is ample material in this book, as well as in the suggested readings, especially the NT, for you to make it all the way to a faith that can actually do something for you. Remember that Christianity offers a total worldview. It attempts to explain the universe, design in nature, consciousness, belief in objective moral values, as well as a realistic appraisal of the condition of man: noble but fallen. It answers the need for justice in this world and assurance of it in the next. The hope it offers for eternal life does not devalue this present life but *enhances* it. It reduces fear and gives meaning. Otherwise, as King Solomon said, "All is vanity" (Ecclesiastes 1:2).

The question is not whether it offers a perfect explanation for all of these, but whether it explains them better than any other competing worldview. The number of options is small and no one has come up with a radically new philosophical system in over 2500 years.

The Christian case is cumulative. It would be exceedingly difficult to bring the system down short of finding the body of Jesus (remember my friend who quipped about not finding Jimmy Hoffa). Christianity has been attacked on a historical or philosophical basis for two thousand years. Christianity has proven robust in light of new findings from the natural sciences, archeology, biblical studies, and ancient history. Christianity and the Bible have been declared dead many times but, as with Jesus, the corpse won't stay down. This book is premised on the idea that since you will be dead for a long time, it is prudent to try to secure the best possible outcome.

But how can you tell whether you would like being with Jesus if you do not know him? Besides, most non-believers (including Gandhi) say they admire Jesus; it is just Christians they don't like. Are you willing to let the words or actions of some small segment of Jesus' followers separate you from God? You may have already decided you dislike the church or its people and you may have all kinds of apprehensions about becoming "one of them." God is not asking you to join the Christian Right or the Republican Party or a particular Christian tradition. Many of you are reacting to perhaps a poorly presented and poorly understood religion of your youth. It's time you reexamined things for yourself. God is asking you into a relationship with his son and a body of believers, whatever the cultural trappings.

Answering the Question of Eternity or What Do You Want?

Follow your heart
Living for the day, forget about tomorrow.
Follow your heart
Any other way can only lead to sorrow.
Follow your heart.

—Triumph, Rock Band[104]

The human heart is most deceitful and desperately wicked. Who really knows how bad it is?

—Jeremiah, Old Testament Prophet (Jeremiah 17:9)

For the gate is wide, and the way is broad that leads to destruction.

—Jesus (Matthew 7:13 NAS)

As we have discussed, the central claim of Christianity is the resurrection of Jesus. This is the core of what the apostles preached starting just fifty days after the event. No bodily resurrection, no Christianity. It's that simple. Unlike other religions and philosophies, the Christian claim is grounded in history—real events in real space and time. The NT claim is that the resurrection of Jesus was witnessed, recorded, and transmitted. These claims are open to the methods of the historian. However, historians deal with

---

104 R. Emmett, G. Moore, M. Levine, *Follow Your Heart* (Song, Universal Music/ MGB, 1984).

probabilities. While there is no absolute certainty from historical inquiry, it *appears* to be true.

The examination of the testimony contained in the Bible and other historical documents appeals to eyewitness testimony. Both the historian and our own legal system have methods to test the credibility of these types of witnesses.

In historical investigations, historians judge the writer of the text against other sources, and how close to the original event the text was written. In the case of the NT, the writers show detailed knowledge of the time and setting of the described events, the proximity of the witnesses, the inclusion of embarrassing details, corroboration by hostile witnesses (James and Paul), and the number and consistency of the early manuscripts.

But what is evidence to one person is often dismissed by another. Is there some objective standard that gets us past our notions of what we are willing to believe? In the philosophical sense, no. All commitments to systems of evidence are faith based worldview commitments. No system can be evaluated by criteria outside the system as was shown in Chapter 4. But our legal system provides a common place to stand and examine the evidence. Fortunately, the Bible's system of witness and testimony *is* the biblical system and so it is a proper means of evaluation. Despite its limitations due to human limits and sin (also acknowledged within the biblical system) it provides a common standard of acceptability. In our criminal justice system, the standard of proof must be "beyond a reasonable doubt" when rendering a verdict. Some of you may think the appeal to eyewitness testimony is weak. We know that legal witnesses can be liars or mistaken. I have already dealt with the "liar" objection of Jesus' own words (C. S. Lewis' famous "lord, liar, lunatic" alternatives). But what of the others who were the witnesses of Jesus' work and words? Let's examine the biblical witness in the legal sense.

It is hard to underestimate the extent of the biblical eyewitness testimony. Someone once calculated that if all of the eyewitness testimony contained in the NT were transcribed in the form of court testimony, it would amount to over 500 hours! Does the eyewitness testimony contained in the Bible hold up to legal scrutiny?

Simon Greenleaf, who wrote the first book of rules regarding the handling of federal evidence for Harvard Law School at the end of the eighteenth century, looked into the reliability of the testimony of the eyewitnesses to the resurrection—the writers of the gospels. He concluded that it was exactly what we should expect given the nature of this type of witness. Greenleaf concluded:

> There is enough of discrepancy to show that there could have been no previous concert among them; and at the same time such substantial agreement as to show that they all were independent narrators of the same great transaction, as the events actually occurred.[105]

The eyewitness testimony to the words and works of Jesus of Nazareth would be admissible in a court of law. Greenleaf was not

---

105 S. Greenleaf, *The Testimony of the Evangelists Examined by the Rules of Evidence Administrated in Courts of Justice.* Quote from Appendix, 1 Para. 34. From an adaptation by W. R. Miller. www.tektonics.org/harmonize/greenharmony.htm

a Christian, but became one after deciding to treat the gospels by the standards of his profession.

From a textual historical sense, we are looking at memory written down during the lifetimes of many eyewitnesses. This provides multiple sources to back-check the writing. From his book *Jesus and the Eyewitnesses,* Richard Bauckham writes:

> The eyewitnesses who remembered the events of the history of Jesus were remembering inherently...unusual events that would have impressed themselves on the memory...landmark or life-changing events for them in many cases, and their memories would have been reinforced and stabilized by frequent rehearsals, beginning soon after the event...We may conclude that the memories of eyewitnesses of the history of Jesus score highly by the criteria for likely reliability that have been established by the psychological study of recollective memory.[106]

But where does this information leave you, the reader? The apostle Paul in 1 Corinthians 15—right after citing his eyewitness testimony—moves immediately to the conclusion that if Christ was raised, we will be too if we are found in Christ. In verse 43 Paul says, "Our bodies now disappoint us, but when they are raised, they will be full of glory. They are weak now, but when they are raised, they will be full of power." We don't know exactly what this means, but doesn't it sound better than the alternative, where those not found in the book of life are thrown into the lake of fire, the second death (Revelation 20:11)? Do you desire the picture of resurrection over the second death? This is the heart of the matter.

---

106 R. Bauckham, *Jesus and the Eyewitnesses: The Gospels as Eyewitness Testimony.* (Grand Rapids, Eerdmans, 2006), 346.

Just because some historical finding can be doubted, would you want to bet against it? Would you want to bet your life savings that Caesar did *not* cross the Rubicon? Likewise, will you bet your eternal destiny that Jesus' tomb was *not* empty on Easter morning, and he did not appear to his followers even though this is the majority report from even non-Christian scholars?[107]

Just as one who sits on a jury must decide, so must you also. But you are not just evaluating historical probabilities and the force of the wager; you are also working out of the desires of your heart.

At this point it may seem I have unfairly loaded up the case: it appears true and it promises the greatest good, so what's the problem? Again, I think this is where the heart comes in, your whole person. But what is stopping you? Going back to the quote from Jeremiah the prophet (Jeremiah 19:17) as to why the heart is desperately wicked, let me give one traditional Christian answer: the world, the flesh, and the devil.

You may not believe in the devil but we know there's a world that is full of things more alluring for our natural selves than Christ. There was a scene in the movie *Moonstruck* where Cher asks a middle-aged man why middle-aged men chase after young women, and he answers offhandedly, "Maybe it's the fear of death." Cher stops dead in her tracks and says, "That's it!"

Point one is the world. As much as we complain about not enough time to get things done, we still look for things to fill up our day to keep us hassled and busy. If we have too much leisure

---

107 For support for this statement see M. Licona's book: *The Resurrection of Jesus.* (Downers Grove, IL, IVP, 2010).

we might spend time in introspection and see what Pascal calls the "infinite abyss" that can only be filled with an infinite God. Pascal writes:

> God alone is man's true good...it is a...fact that nothing in nature has been found to take his place.[108]
>
> Being unable to cure death, wretchedness and ignorance, men have decided, in order to be happy, not to think about such things.[109]

In other words, diversion is a great barrier to seeking God.

A second major factor Pascal notes is indifference. He noted in his writing the appearance of indifference towards one's fate after death as a character flaw, "...to be carried off limply to my death, uncertain of my future state for all eternity... Who would wish to have as his friend a man who argued like that?"[110] Yet today the level of indifference is higher than perhaps any other time in history, with the possible exception of the late Roman empire, which was decadent, sophisticated, skeptical, relativistic, and promiscuous (which I guess is a type of diversion).

We are so afraid of caring about truth that we approach the big questions with a big "Whatever." In John 16:37, Jesus says, "Everyone on the side of truth listens to me." When Pontius Pilate asks Jesus the question, "What is truth?" you can almost see the little cartoon bubble forming over Pilate's head, "Whatever."

Today's proliferation of information breeds skepticism. A quick search of Google, for instance, can yield a plethora of opinions and

---

108 B. Pascal, *Pensees,* trans. A. J. Krailsheimer, (New York, Penguin, 1995), 45.

109 Ibid., 8.

110 Ibid., 130.

purported refutations of every argument I've made. Those who are seeking a way to avoid belief may grasp at any argument, no matter how weak, to support their misplaced desires. Though I'm sure I've made some mistakes in presenting the Christian case, merely reading a purported refutation can never replace a careful weighing of the *total* evidence. If you've been tempted to do this, have you spent as much effort looking to support it?

Many sincere people wonder about how the God of the Bible will treat people who have not heard the gospel or who are sincere believers in other religions. But perhaps a more interesting question is how will that God treat those who have heard the message, but responded with sheer indifference to the case for Christ? Why shouldn't indifference be morally culpable before God? Before one gets too worked up about the fate of the lost in outermost Wherever, it may be helpful to ask a few questions closer to home.

If this message is true, and I'm indifferent to that potential, what will be my end? Pascal was outraged by the indifference of the leisure class of seventeenth century France. He writes, "Thus the fact that there exist men who are indifferent to the loss of their being and the peril of an eternity of wretchedness is against nature."[111] I want to shake people and say, can't you even bother to look? Bertrand Russell, a famous Atheist of the 1950s, said that if he finds himself before God on judgment day, he would say in his defense, "Not enough evidence!" Can you honestly say even that much?

Pascal goes on to give a reason for what I will call *apparent* indifference. I say apparent because I believe that indifference is

---

111 Ibid., 131.

a mask for fear. Pascal wrote that men loath religion, they fear it might be true. On this topic Peter Kreeft explains it is as if you were trying to "...feed spinach to a reluctant baby who stubbornly closes his mouth... What you have to do is make the baby *hungry*."[112] That is why I quoted St. Paul regarding the nature of our new resurrected bodies.

Philosopher Peter Kreeft, in his wonderful commentary on Pascal called *Christianity for Modern Pagans* writes, "God's claim is that 'you will find me when you seek me with all your heart'" (Jeremiah 29:13).[113] This claim is not refuted unless tested. We must do our part of the experiment by seeking with the heart, in other words our innermost being: the mind, will, and emotions. Therefore Christianity can never be refuted by one who is indifferent, no matter how intelligent he is. Kreeft goes on to write:

> Hell is not populated mainly by passionate rebels but by nice, bland, indifferent, respectable people who never gave a damn...How could anyone act as if it made no difference whether the obscure path through the dark forest of life leads home or into quicksand; whether the waterslide has a pool at the bottom or rocks? It is insanity to sing, "I don't care" while walking along such a path.[114]

My father told me he was indifferent as to whether he went to heaven or hell. I told him that was an absurd statement. The day he collapsed from a stroke, the neighbor who attended him said he was terrified. She related to me that, in her words, "This was a man

---

112 P. Kreeft, *Christianity for Modern Pagans* (San Francisco, Ignatius, 1993), 31.

113 Ibid., 197.

114 Ibid., 196-197.

who knew he was going to meet his maker." I had been praying for a moment like this and what I would do if it came. I was prepared by prayer for the opening that God's providence provided.

As I had asked, God left my father with enough faculties that he could understand the message of saving faith and respond to it. In the hospital, I got a chance to talk and pray with him over the next several days. Here is a case of someone who said he didn't care about his eternal destiny; but when facing death he *did* care. My father was blessed that God gave him this final chance to hear the message of saving faith. In the end, my father accepted Christ as his savior. So it is clear that my father had a heart that did desire the "beatitude" (Pascal's word for blessing) of eternal life.

The timing of the whole incident with my father, the fact that I was visiting him, along with a cluster of other circumstances, has made me certain that my prayers in the preceding months had made a difference. When we stare death in the face, some will grab the rope of salvation, others will delude themselves with distractions, and some will stay defiant until the end.

What I Think I Have Shown

• • •

In Chapters 1 and 2, I pointed out the obvious that something happens when you die, even if you just rot. I tried to get you to think about other possibilities, including being judged by a perfect and righteous God, who has in his mercy provided a way for you to stand before him and be judged not guilty. I hope this possibility will be taken seriously because we all have skin in the game.

To take this possibility seriously, one must have the proper mental machinery or worldview. In Chapters 3 and 4, I discussed some of the factors that go into the makeup of a worldview: what you believe is ultimately real and how you know this to be the case. Forming a worldview should be done with thoughtful deliberation, yet is seldom done. Usually our worldview is a subconscious set of control beliefs picked up from our surroundings and is influenced by our desires. A worldview is hard to change. Forming an ultimate commitment is particularly dangerous. Vern Poythress, PhD (Harvard) observes the outworking of worldview thinking expressed in Chapter 4. He notes that anyone who evaluates religion must have criteria for that evaluation. That criterion must be, knowingly or not, more ultimate than the religion he is evaluating. This may lead, in some cases, to evaluating religion from the standpoint of science. But your choice of science to evaluate religion is just an expression of your own autonomy; you are doing the evaluating from the standpoint of yourself, your own standards of reasonableness. This may be done with some critical reflection but more often it is based on nothing more than how something rubs you. Dr. Tim Keller said in a sermon that we have plenty of evidence that we are not competent to run our own lives. To have yourself as a norm (law) is really a commitment to live without norms. I know this first hand because several of my friends have told me so. I did it myself. The bad news is we are all like this, the Bible tells us so. The good news is that God sent his son to save us from the prison of ourselves.

In Chapters 5–7, I presented evidence for a Theistic/Christian worldview. I demonstrated that an immaterial being created everything we call the universe out of nothing but his will. I showed that a cluster of arguments, both philosophical and scientific, point to this conclusion. Among them is the principle of sufficient reason: the universe requires an explanation. And the argument from contingency: the universe does not contain an explanation for itself and must have an outside cause. I then took a more in-depth look at what is known as the Kalam cosmological argument that showed why the universe cannot be the product of an infinite chain of material causes but must start with an immaterial cause that possesses intentionality. This cause has the attributes of the God of the Bible.

We can also see the personhood of God in the design of the universe: this includes the physical laws of nature, the fine tuning of the physical constants, the origin of biological information, and the fact that we are made up of irreducibly complex "machines" that must have full function from the beginning with no possibility of gradual or evolutionary assembly. An impersonal designer is just not an intelligible idea. You will find these arguments, when viewed from the standpoint of faith seeking understanding, to fit the Christian worldview. Doing science—or for that matter, spirituality—without a personal God as a reference point leaves you hanging with feet firmly planted in midair. In using arguments from philosophy, science, or history, I am not suggesting we judge the truth of God by some criteria chosen by us. I am suggesting that when all of these ways of knowing fit, then we can have certainty that Christianity is true as no other system coheres this well across all human experience.

In Part III, Chapters 8–11 I look at the following question: in a God-created universe, did God reveal himself to sentient beings that he purposed? This is obviously a real possibility, given omnipotence, but did this actually happen? It is clear that Jesus of Nazareth claimed to be from God and of God. He validated this fantastic claim by rising from the dead. The historical set of facts surrounding this event—his death, his burial, his empty tomb, and his many post mortem appearances to friend and foe alike—are nearly certain. It would have been impossible for his followers to proclaim his resurrection in Jerusalem just fifty days after the event if it were not true, as all these doings were very public. As St. Paul said, they were not done in a corner.

I gave evidence that the God of the universe is behind the Hebrew/Christian Bible. Many of its events were foretold in advance, especially those concerning the coming Jewish Messiah and the new covenant God would institute for the whole world. Finally, Jesus himself predicted the end of the Jewish age in one generation after his death with the destruction of the temple and the city. This was incomprehensible to his followers when he said it, but it happened right on schedule in one generation. The dates are firm and so there is no possibility it was made up after the fact. This knowledge of the future requires that God be outside of time, as the cosmological argument in Chapter 5 requires. This confirms that the God of creation and the God of the Bible are the same. This material narrows down who God is. It is the Christian God, the God of grace, who comes down (condescends) to reveal himself in a manner we can understand. This is the God who saves.

Then finally, I discussed in Part IV, Chapters 12–16 the philosophical objections, the problem of evil and the objection that the universe is just too big. I believe I have disarmed these as logical defeaters for the Christian God, but I have no control over how you react to them. I ask again that they be taken from the standpoint of "faith seeking understanding."

I've presented what amounts to a cumulative case for the Christian faith; my απολογια or "apologia" from the Greek language, which, translated into English, is my "defense" of the Christian faith. This cumulative case is sufficient for all who desire God.

Two Faith Journeys: What Does It Look Like?

● ● ●

ntony Flew was born in 1923, the son of a British Methodist minister. He grew up believing what he was taught, but never felt "connected" to God. By age fifteen he was beginning to doubt the whole thing. In college he became an Atheist and was attracted to Marxism. His initial Atheism grew out of the presence of evil in the world. He drifted into philosophy and eventually developed the most sophisticated arguments for Atheism since David Hume (see the discussion in Chapter 8). As a member of the Socratic club he locked horns with the great Christian apologist C. S. Lewis and seemed at times to have Lewis flummoxed. When the BBC recently asked Flew if he had absolutely refuted Lewis' Christian apologetic, Flew explained, "No, I just didn't believe there was sufficient reason for believing it."[115] Such was Flew's case in the presumption of Atheism.

Flew continued his interest in philosophy of religion because it would be "madly imprudent" to be on the wrong side of the gods. (Does this sound like Pascal?) Flew wrote: "…any scientifically minded person must want to discover what, if anything, it is possible to know about these matters."[116] It seems that Flew was

---

115 A. Flew, *There is a God* (New York, Harper One, 2007), 24.
116 Ibid., 29.

also positively influenced by C. S. Lewis's Socratic club and the Socratic principle of following the evidence wherever it may lead; this became a guiding principle for Flew throughout his life.

On the other side of the pond, American philosopher Alvin Plantinga had developed the argument that belief in God was "properly basic," and absent some defeater like the problem of evil, there was rational warrant for believing in God. When Flew and Plantinga debated in 1985, it was a standoff, neither side was willing to concede burden of proof. Alvin Plantinga claimed belief in God was "properly basic," and Antony Flew held ground on a similar claim of an assumption of Atheism. According to Flew, neither side moved the ball.[117]

In a subsequent debate with Flew, Bill Craig used the "free will defense" (perfected by Plantinga) to effect and Flew recognized for the first time that his defeater for the existence of God had been undercut. It is somewhat surprising this took so long. Flew had been arguing against the reformed (Calvinist) view that God predestines all things, including free choices. Flew wrote, "I had always been repulsed by the doctrine of predestination, which holds that God predestines the damnation of most human beings."[118] This got Flew thinking but it still didn't overcome the presumption of Atheism. What could?

In 2004 Flew went to NY to debate with Israeli scientist Gerald Schroeder among others, on the topic of the evidence for the existence of God. Schroeder argued against the "monkey theorem":

---

117 Ibid., 70.
118 Ibid., 73.

enough monkeys typing long enough will eventually write a sonnet. This has been the basis for naturalistic scenarios to explain the origins of life. To the surprise of all present, Flew announced that he now accepted the existence of *a* God. So what began as a debate became an open discussion on modern scientific discoveries that point to a higher intelligence.

Flew posed a question to his former fellow Atheists "What would have to occur…to constitute for a reason to at least consider the existence of a superior Mind?"[119] But in his book, Flew shows the scientific support for the "mind of God," in his words, "…emerges from the conceptual heart of modern science and imposes itself on the rational mind"[120], yet Flew gives examples of scientists that for the most part are those who remain Agnostic on the ideal of a personal savior in Jesus Christ.

However Flew was not a Christian and did not believe in revelation—that God personally reveals himself in scripture or Jesus. Flew defended what he called "the God of Aristotle."[121] It would be accurate to say that Flew was a Deist; in his own words, this for him was not a faith journey but "…a pilgrimage of reason."[122]

So why did Flew stay stuck with Deism? One might imagine that given Flew's need for sufficient evidence he simply rejected the evidence for the resurrection of Jesus and other miracles as insufficient to clear the bar of skepticism as he set it. After all, he

---

119 Ibid., 88.

120 Ibid., 112.

121 Ibid., 93.

122 Ibid., 93 and also 155.

resisted the cosmological and design arguments until others stated them in a form that proved irresistible to an honest intellect. Did the NT evidence fail to rise to this level?

It would seem in Flew's own words from his book that he has fallen into the C. S. Lewis "lord, liar, lunatic" conundrum, as he does not consider the fact that Jesus is anything but a mere "charismatic figure."[123] However, in Appendix B in his book is a short dialog written by Bishop N. T. Wright on Jesus and the resurrection. Flew prefaces this passage by stating "If you are wanting Omnipotence to set up a religion, this is the one to beat."[124] Although Flew was doubtful that the resurrection happened, he found it important enough to include N. T. Wright's thoughts on this subject in his book.

Flew had reasoned to God from nature, and now he was starting to take a look at specific Christian claims from a historical perspective. He obviously found something worthy in Wright's take on Jesus and the resurrection. But something else was going on. A clue to this might be hidden within an interesting parable Flew presents in his book.

He tells us of an island isolated from civilization. A satellite phone washes up on the beach that still works. The natives play with the buttons, make connections, and hear voices. The cleverest of the tribe, the scientists, manage to build a replica and when they push the same buttons they get the voices. The obvious conclusion is that they have made a voice box that makes human sounds but these voices are just properties of the device.

---

123 Ibid., 157.
124 Ibid., 186.

But the tribal sage announces that on deep reflection that the voices coming out of the box are from people like themselves. But the scientists protest. They note that when they damage part of the setup, it no longer works so the voices are only properties of the parts that they put together. At this point, Flew is trying to get his fellow Atheists to think outside their preconceived ideas.[125] I note that this is the standard take on the brain and personhood from neuroscience.

Now we fast forward to the end of the book. Flew has assembled his case for the existence of a being like the God of the Bible: all-present, all-powerful, and all-knowing. He says he is open to learning more and points us to his Appendix B and Bishop Wright's case for Jesus and the resurrection. But then he takes us back to the parable of the satellite phone that ended with the sage being ridiculed by the scientists. Flew says,

> Let us imagine it ending differently. The scientists adopt as a working hypothesis the sage's suggestion that the phone is a medium of contact with other humans...they now accept that other human beings are out there...they know they are not alone.[126]

My Faith Journey[127]

Like Antony Flew, as a child I believed in God. It was a source of comfort to me after my mother died when I was ten. By high school I was deeply committed to science, the only subject I was

125 Ibid., 85-86.

126 Ibid., 158.

127 Paul Ernst, "Evidence That Produced a Verdict," *Challenger Magazine*, vol. 45, no. 1 (Jan-Mar, 2006), 12-15.

really good at. Scientists became role models and I was uncritically absorbing their worldview. I suspect most of us operate this way. I was also under the influence of a college age friend and his commitment to Ayn Rand's philosophy of Objectivism, which was really just naive Materialism coupled with Libertarian Capitalism that I got from my dad. I never considered myself to be a dogmatic Atheist for at that time scientists were not like the high profile Atheists today. But religion seemed silly next to science, and besides, I wanted to be like the smart people.

When I was approached by a "smart guy" (hey, he had a law degree) about the claims of Christ in my early fifties I was becoming aware of my mortality and was willing to listen. Through his thirty page legal brief defending the divinity of Christ, I saw enough to know that the Christian case was a real possibility and I grasped the implications immediately. I saw that I would have to make a decision for or against Christianity. There was no in between.

What followed was an eighteen-month intensive investigation of the truth claims of Christianity, and I knew that centered on the resurrection of Jesus, and supporting issues like OT prophecies. Because I didn't see the Bible as authoritative, I looked to human authority to verify it. God must have been guiding the process. As it turned out, the books I read were very helpful, including *The Case for Christ* by Lee Strobel.

I was impressed that Strobel, a hardheaded Atheist bent on de-converting his wife, could be convinced by evidence that Christianity was true. With my prior commitment to science and with no knowledge whatever of philosophy, I brought a certain common sense realism to the project. Science made me appreciate that the Christian claim was backed by evidence and not just blind faith. Fortunately I had never been fully indoctrinated into a belief in scientific Naturalism, the commitment that miracles are deemed impossible from the outset. Besides, I actually wanted Christianity to be true. So I confess that a certain "selection bias" was working in the sources I chose to study. I only realized later that that this was the work of the Holy Spirit.

However, I had a deep need for intellectual integrity—perhaps it was just pretension or plain old pride. But to fulfill this need, I felt compelled to check out the opposition.

Sometimes I would go for weeks on end between Christian and Atheist web sites. Some of these sites had the work of people I once admired, like Isaac Asimov. His Atheist "Bible" pointed out all the alleged contradictions in the Christian Bible. My heart sank while reading some of this stuff. I didn't know if these authors were right, but I kept trying to find answers. Over time I gradually drilled down through the layers of argument and began to discern some basic truths. Writers like Asimov were simply regurgitating the old higher critics and trading off their cachet with a hip new audience. The case for the resurrection of Jesus became more solid with study, and most of the Bible difficulties the popular writers traffic in had standard answers by real biblical scholars or involved issues of interpretation that did not affect core beliefs.

After months of looking at claim and counterclaim, I began to realize I was coming around full circle. Both sides were covering the same ground. Either there was a reliable chain of witnesses to the Easter events or there wasn't. It came down to which system of evidence I was willing to commit to. It was time to make a decision.

I finally started reading the Bible for myself and between the picture of Christ in the OT (Isaiah 52:13-53 in particular) and the ring of truth in the NT, I saw the truth of the story and soon after prayed to the person of Jesus Christ to be my living lord and savior in accordance with the scripture that says, *"That if you confess with your mouth Jesus as Lord, and believe in your heart that God raised Him from the dead, you shall be saved"* (Romans 10:9).

Antony Flew and I both decided to follow the evidence. Why did I end up as a believer and as far as we know, he didn't? Flew's commitment to follow the evidence and his intellectual integrity are impressive (unlike many of the new Atheists: Hitchens, Dawkins, Dennett, and Harris). Even though Flew believed as a child, he said it was simply assent to what his father and peers believed. He never needed God in any personal way. He pursued the truth as he saw it, but he never pursued God. He only came to believe in God's existence when the facts compelled him. After this admission he made statements that he had no interest in eternal life and once dead wished to stay dead. I think that makes all the difference. God has set eternity in our hearts but sometimes it dies. Jesus talked about people who receive the good news, but then let other things choke it out, so that it never grows (see Matthew 13). Flew talks about it being prudent to be on the right side of the gods, but the force of the wager seems to have been lost on him. I think I know one reason.

It has been made known to me that Flew was repulsed by the notion of hell and didn't want anything to do with such a system—a system where a supposedly loving God would torture people forever in hell. It would seem that Flew was still trying to conform God to his standards and had not come to terms with God's purity, holiness, and sovereignty.

But I think he had an unnecessary stumbling block. Like most people, he had absorbed popular notions of hell that are more medieval than Biblical. When a threat becomes more horrifying than one can internalize, one is inclined to dismiss it (see Appendix II "*Is Hell as Hot as It Used to Be?*"). In the spirit of the Reformation (always reforming within the bounds of scripture), I put forth what I believe is a Biblical alternative view of God's justice (as opposed to Dante's *Inferno*) and perhaps remove a stumbling block.

At the end of Flew's book, he states, "Some claim to have made contact with this Mind [his idea of God]. I have not—yet… Someday I might hear a Voice that says, 'can you hear me now?'"[128] I don't know exactly what Flew was expecting to hear or how literally he took the idea of hearing God's voice. God actually speaking to a person is infrequent even in the Bible. God can directly speak to a person, and I believe he does speak today, but many times this is in a frontier situation like in Muslim countries that are without the Bible and dreams and visions are necessary as in OT times. God's more normal operation is that he speaks to us through his written word, the Bible. That is why he oversaw its production.

The answer to why some people believe and some don't is to be found somewhere between man's will and God's will. When I read scripture, it had the ring of truth. Apparently when Flew read

---

128 Ibid., 158.

scripture it did not speak to him the same way. God really doesn't want anyone to perish, and he has revealed himself by special revelation in the Bible. So have you done your part?

What Must I Do to Be Saved?

So you have looked at some of the evidence and you understand the logic of the wager. How do you move on to a "saving faith"?

An analogy of faith that is a step up from the wager, but not unrelated, is to imagine you are being chased by a bear, but you are heading towards the edge of a cliff. There is a branch that is strong enough to hold you, you must go over the side and you must grab the branch or you will be lost. Tim Keller writes:

> If your mind is filled with intellectual certainty that the branch can support you, but you don't actually reach out and grab it, you are lost. If your mind is instead filled with doubts and uncertainty that the branch can hold you, but you reach out and grab it anyway, you will be saved. Why? It is not the strength of your faith but the object of your faith that actually saves you. Strong faith in a weak branch is fatally inferior to weak faith in a strong branch.[129]

This story illustrates the nature of a forced decision and the fact that it is not how much faith we have but what or in whom we put our faith.

Perhaps a better example is an old story about the Great Blondin, a tightrope walker and showman from long ago. Blondin loved to work the crowds at Niagara Falls. With a rope strung from side to

---

129 T. Keller, *The Reason for God: Belief in an Age of Skepticism* (New York, Riverhead Books, 2008), 245.

side above the falls, he'd thrill the crowds with his ability to walk the wire carrying various loads. One time he pulled out a wheelbarrow and asked the crowd if they believed he could push it across the chasm. They all shouted, "Yes!" When he succeeded with that he next asked the crowd whether they believed he could carry a load of bricks in the wheelbarrow. Again, they shouted, "Yes!" When he once again returned he asked whether they believed he could carry a man across in the wheelbarrow. The level of excitement was palpable. They shouted, "Yes!" Blondin asked the crowd who would volunteer to step into the wheelbarrow to go across the falls with him? This time the crowd remained silent.[130]

As long as belief involved risk to others only, the crowd was all for it. When the risk became more personal, each had a different reaction. That's the biblical definition of *believe*—a level of trust that is up close and very personal. And this is the level of trust God seeks. Are you willing to trust Jesus with your whole life even though you do not fully understand what that means?

"Okay," you say, "I would like to believe what you wrote, but I still have doubts." When Mary Magdalene went to Jesus' tomb early Easter morning and found it empty she ran back to Peter and said, "They have taken away the Lord out of the tomb and we do not know where they laid him." Mary leapt to a non-supernatural conclusion—grave robbing.

She had held out the hope that Jesus was the one who would redeem Israel. Her faulty assumptions lead her to the wrong conclusion about the facts in front of her. But then Peter and John

---

130 A reference to this story can be found here: www.jesusisthelight.net/BLONDIN.htm

went into the tomb and saw the collapsed wrappings and the head napkin neatly folded up (see Appendix I, The Shroud of Turin). They saw and believed. They returned to their homes believing.

Mary continued to wait outside the tomb. When Jesus appeared to her, she thought it was the gardener and said "Sir, if you have carried him away, tell me where you have laid him." She was still making an assumption based on the first century Jewish belief that resurrection of the dead would not happen until the end of the world. Then Jesus said to her, "Mary," and her whole world changed. Jesus was alive. Her first assumption was wrong. What she had hoped for proved reliable now. *This* branch had not broken.

So if you have doubt, look and see what is behind the doubt. Have you made assumptions? It is not faith versus reason but faith versus faith, assumption versus assumption, and belief versus belief.

This does not mean everything is up for grabs. Some faith commitments are better than others, not just in terms of being true but also in what they promise. Can they deliver what you hope for?

At this point fear can set in. It does for me. I know what is at the bottom of this fear; it's too good to be true. But is that an argument based on reason? It is instead based on experience. We all know that there is no pot of gold at the end of the rainbow, Cinderella stays too long at the ball, and the frog is still a frog. My investment in that sure thing didn't work. My heart still doesn't pump right. What I'm saying is I agree; we all thought we knew the answer, but we were wrong.

This is the difference between the world's truth and God's truth.

"What is faith? It is the confident assurance that what we hope for is going to happen. It is the evidence of things we cannot yet see" (Hebrews 11:1). Hope sustains faith despite the circumstances. Mary Magdalene never stopped calling Jesus the Lord. She was hoping he was the one true savior. Her hope did not fuel her belief. The facts fueled her belief, and her belief fueled her hope.

We need to doubt our doubts and reach out and grab that branch. When we need assurance, we need to gaze at the empty tomb. The majority of NT scholars of all stripes believe that Jesus' tomb was empty that first Easter morning. Most do not believe that grave robbery is an adequate explanation. Yet only a few put their trust in Christ. The Christian faith is not just assent to the facts given here. To go beyond intellectual assent you must know why Jesus died. He died for you so that you could be wrapped in his righteousness, not your own, and thereby made acceptable to a perfect and holy God. It is a gift, as is the faith needed to accept it.

So why not settle the question of your eternity now? When St. Paul was imprisoned for a disturbance in Philippi, an earthquake broke open the jail and the jailer was impressed that Paul and his God were behind it. He cried out to Paul, "What must I do to be saved?" Paul replied, "Believe in the lord Jesus and you and your household will be saved." The word "household" may be relevant for some of you at this point. You may have a hidden desire not to be saved because of loved ones you fear may be left behind. I don't think Paul is saying that just because the jailer believed, his household will be automatically included. Paul is saying that they will be saved by seeing the jailer's faith. If you have loved ones, the best thing you can do for them is to become a believer and point them to Christ.

There are many salvation verses in the NT, which is one reason to read it completely. One such chain used by evangelists like Billy Graham is as follows:

Romans 3:23: "For all have sinned; all fall short of God's glorious standard. Yet now God in his gracious kindness declares us not guilty. He has done this through Christ Jesus, who has freed us by taking away our sins and to satisfy God's anger against us."

Then in Romans 6:23 it says, "For the wages of sin is death, but the free gift of God is eternal life through Christ Jesus our Lord.

Romans 5:8 completes the thought: "But God showed his great love for us by sending Christ to die for us while we were still sinners."

We find out why in John 3:16: "For God so loved the world that He gave his only Son, so that whoever believes in him shall not perish but have eternal life."

Salvation that comes from trusting Christ, which is the message we preach, is already in easy reach. The scriptures say, "The message is close at hand; it is on your lips and in your heart. For if you confess with your mouth that Jesus is Lord and believe in your heart that God raised him from the dead, you will be saved." (Romans 10:9)

If you say this with conviction, you have passed from death to life.

Is it that simple? Yes and no. One must understand what it means for Jesus to be lord. Jesus cannot be your savior without being your lord. This means that you are in agreement with him that he has authority over every aspect of your life. It means that you have repented of the practice of sin and have changed your mind and turned to him. It also means you are not ashamed of him. It means you are willing to tell others you believe in him. The Christian faith is not private, even though political correctness says it should be. This does not mean that once saved we do these things perfectly, but at minimum we must be willing to agree with Jesus. We must be willing to turn from sin as God defines it, and allow him to have access to every area of our lives. This is a process that is not finished this side of heaven.

I will be praying for each person who reads this. I want you to be in my family forever—the family of God our father and the lord Jesus Christ.

SUGGESTED READING

● ● ●

General Interest

* *The Reason for God*, Tim Keller.
  T. Keller, *The Reason for God: Belief in an Age of Skepticism*
  (New York, Riverhead Books, 2008)

This pastor has built a huge church in Manhattan among a tough crowd—sophisticates who read *The New Yorker*. It covers all the bases.

* *Mere Christianity*, C. S. Lewis.
  C. S. Lewis, *Mere Christianity* (San Francisco, Harper Collins, 2001).

This little book is perhaps the most important work for the general reader in the last fifty years. It centers on the moral argument, which is where most of us live our lives, and why Christianity is necessary for a moral universe. Short, but pithy.

* *The God Question,* J. P. Moreland.
  J. P. Moreland, *The God Question: An Invitation to a Life of Meaning*, (Redmond, WA, Conversant Media Group, 2009).

Short and readable. It goes to the head and the heart. A book I wish I could have written.

- *The Case for Christ*, Lee Strobel.
  Lee Strobel, *The Case for Christ: A Journalist's Personal Investigation of the Evidence for Jesus*, (Grand Rapids, MI, Zondervan, 1998).

This chronicles the journey to faith by an investigative reporter who was upset by his wife's conversion. He sets out to use his skills to debunk Christianity; two years later he can offer no excuse not to believe it. He uses a breezy style of interviews with top scholars. He focuses on NT reliability and the resurrection.

Advanced Science and Philosophy

- *Reasonable Faith*, William Lane Craig.
  William Lane Craig, *Reasonable Faith: Christian Truth and Apologetics* 3rd ed, (Wheaton, IL, Crossway Books, 2008).

I know Bill Craig, and one immediately gets the impression that he is the smartest guy in the room. The book is accessible but not easy. It goes into more depth with the arguments I have made for the existence of God and the resurrection. Dr. Craig is equally at home addressing the Soviet Academy of Science or his Baptist Sunday school class. He is a gifted philosopher and evangelist. He ends his tour de force with a touching story about how he came to faith in Christ as a disaffected teenager, won over by the girl in the next seat in high school. Dr. Craig's work is a perfect example of loving the Lord with all your heart *and* your mind. A slightly more popular version is called *On Guard*.

And, of Course...the Bible

Above all other books, the Bible will give you the direct message, unfiltered by the traditions of men. Besides some interesting history and wisdom, the words contain the life of the spirit and can save the souls of the willing. I would suggest a study Bible with notes, especially for reading the old testament. The *New International Version (NIV)* translation is the most used dynamic translation—conveying thought for thought, not word for word. You can get most Bible translations with study notes in line with your interests: apologetics, archeology, men, women, and teenagers—you name it. I use the *Life Application Bible*, which is balanced in this respect. I have used the *New Living Translation* in this book as the default translation for its readability and faithfulness to transmitting the intended concepts—not an easy combination.

I do not like the politically correct trend to gender neutrality present in some of the more recent translations, which distorts how God wants to present himself. (Besides, in spite of the masculine articles and pronouns that the Bible uses to refer to God, Genesis 1:27 makes it very clear that both men and women are made in God's image.)

Although it misses a few words we now know from recent manuscript discoveries, if you appreciate the language, then nothing beats the *King James Version (KJV)*. Some Biblical passages just do not sound right any other way. You can get the same flow and accuracy from the *New King James (NKJV)*.

Best of the Web

APOLOGETICS 315: www.apologetics315.com

This website contains work by many of the scholars I have mentioned. It has links to most of the helpful web sites I could mention as well as articles, pod casts, and interviews.

STAND TO REASON: www.str.org

Teaches critical thinking, with strong commentary on moral relativism and religious pluralism. It includes information about how to think through ethical issues and how to be an ambassador for Christ in a modern (and postmodern) society.

THE DISCOVERY INSTITUTE: www.discovery.org

Evolution and intelligent design. Not strictly Christian but the go-to place for all things ID. Offers many contributing scholars and viewpoints, including non-Christian contributors who just don't buy the party line of Materialist science. I support this organization as they are the public whipping boy of Materialist science and a lot of Christians (on both the left and right) don't like the Discovery Institute either. They must be doing something right!

REASONS TO BELIEVE: www.reasons.org

I don't buy their sometimes forced harmonization of science and the Bible, but when it comes to astronomy and planetary science, no one does it better than Dr. Hugh Ross. He provides the ultimate argument for a "just right" universe.

Appendix I. The Shroud of Turin: A Snapshot of the Resurrection or Middle-Age hoax?

● ● ●

Almost anyone glancing at the image below knows exactly what this is supposed to be; the image depicts the crucified Christ. But what exactly is it?

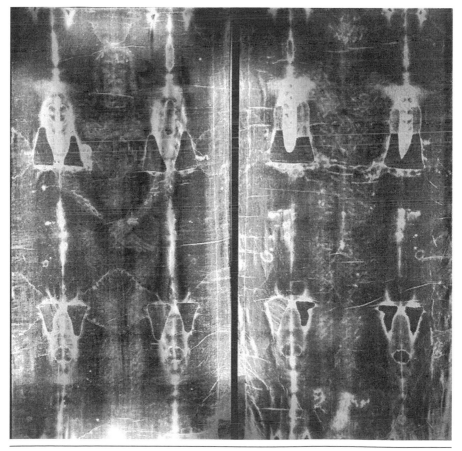

Figure 5. The Shroud of Turin

That question is one of the greatest archeological and scientific mysteries of all time.

The image of the man in the shroud serves as a kind of ink blot test for what one is willing to believe or assume. To confuse matters further, dozens of books have been written and hundreds of Internet postings are devoted to the subject. Numerous television specials have been aired and major media have reported that some finding confirms one claim or another. With the conflicting science and belief systems, can anyone hope to cut through the fog? You have to start by asking the right questions.

Is it real? This can mean two things. Is it really the burial cloth of Jesus? If so, was it made by a natural or supernatural process? Is it an artistic creation intended as a hoax? Or worse, was someone intentionally crucified to make it appear authentic?

One way to approach this is to determine what the shroud is not. It is not a painting or rubbing or a scorching of a cloth draped over a solid figure. It is not from a decomposition of a body under a cloth, either natural or staged. It is not the product of any known process, ancient or modern. Thirty years of attempts by amateurs and professionals have failed to reproduce the unusual characteristics of the image on the cloth. Some attempts have come close on some of the features, but close doesn't count. To be a candidate, any theory must accommodate *all* of the shroud's characteristics. The mystery remains.

Looking at the frontal view, the long parallel marks are from a fire in the Middle Ages. The scalp wounds are consistent with the type of thorns found near Jerusalem that could have been used as a crown. The blood from the scalp appears to be on the hair, but this is an effect of the geometry of the cloth draped over a curved body and flattened out. This was discovered by poking holes in the cloth draped model and flattening the cloth. This characteristic of the image is part of Dr. John Jackson's cloth-collapse model, which is foundational to the geometry of the image.

There is a bruise on the cheek and the wrists are pierced, not the hands. The gospels say that Jesus was struck in the face as close inspection indicates. The pierced wrists are important because Catholic art from the Middle Ages has Jesus depicted as having nails in his hands. This is not anatomically possible as nails in the hands will not support the body weight. The space between the wrist bones is adequate for support. A medieval forger would not have known this, because this was only recently discovered on the skeletons of actual victims from the first century.

The back view also shows the crown of thorns. The most striking feature is the scourge marks administered from both sides in a downward and diagonal direction. The hundreds of marks each correspond to the lead balls on the Roman flagrum that was used for this type of punishment.

The four centimeter chest wound is consistent with a standard Roman lance. The thumbs are not visible, consistent with a crushed ulnar nerve.

In 1978 scientists discovered that the computerized image contains three dimensions encoded on a two-dimensional cloth. This discovery was made possible by a NASA technology designed to image objects in space, such as craters on the moon. Space probe radars are designed to read the light and dark as distance, with the lighter being closer.

When the cloth was imaged in this way, it revealed three-dimensional information. The computer correctly processed the shroud image because the body image falls off to zero when the cloth is four centimeters from the body. By contrast, when a regular 2-D photo is put through the NASA imager, a distortion results. This fact alone should rule out any thought of artistic creation.

Another intriguing feature is that the image is only projected vertically and consists of pixels like a TV or newspaper's black dots on a background. This means that the image was coded in the vertical straight-line direction from the body to the cloth. This feature at first led to talk about miniature lasers pointing upward in the vertical direction. So no matter how the cloth was sloped, the image would always be produced in the vertical plane. This would account for the falloff in intensity as you leave the horizontal plane and move to the vertical, as if the cloth passed over the sides of the body. This would explain the reason that there is not an abrupt demarcation on the sides of the body. The image just fades out as it goes vertical at the sides of the body.

The linen cloth itself has the type of weave found in first century Palestine. The image itself, a pale yellow color, only resides on the top-most fibrils like the hair on one's arm. All fibers have the same color intensity. The apparent intensity is due to the number of fibrils coated as if it were digital! The color consists only of oxidized cellulose, like a newspaper left out the sun. This entails an irradiative process, not a chemical one.

The blood on the shroud is human, type AB. It corresponds perfectly to the wounds and the directional flows consistent with the angles of the arms and body on the cross. The blood does not blot out as expected on a bandage, there is no capillary flow. It did not peel off when the body was removed from the shroud like you would expect when removing a bandage, leaving the question of how the body got out of the shroud while keeping the blood flows in perfect shape. Also the image is not encoded under the blood, showing the image was made after the body was placed on the cloth.

The pollen on the shroud is consistent with Palestine in the spring and the cloths' alleged transit through the Middle East to Edessa in Turkey. From that time in history, the appearance of Jesus' face depicted in art changed. Jesus' first depictions in local art went from a clean shaven Roman face to something like we expect to see now.

Everywhere the shroud is alleged to have traveled, the art depicting Jesus in each area, though varied, was found to collectively contain over forty points of correspondence. In other words, it's clear that all the artists were using a common source. The shroud's known history begins in the 1350s in Constantinople. It radio-carbon dates (C14) to approximately that time and that is the problem.

In principle, carbon dating of an object several thousand years old can be accurate within about fifty years. In practice, carbon dating can be highly inaccurate. For example, a living snail shell was dated to 26,000 years old; one-year-old leaves were dated to 400 years old; and a Viking horn was dated to the future year of 2006. Many more examples can be given. The ratio of radioactive carbon 14 to the naturally occurring carbon 12 is approximately one part in one trillion. So if there are any errors in the small amount of C 14, the date could change dramatically.

Even if the two isotopes are correctly measured, the isotopes measured must be original and must belong only to the object from which they were taken. Any exchange with the environment can have a dramatic effect, and we know that the shroud was subjected to fire, water damage, handling, bacterial coatings, and many other influences.

Carbon from other sources may easily be trapped in porous materials and removal of the contaminant source from the pore spaces and the fissures is almost impossible. The possibility of contamination should be exhaustively investigated and pretreatment measures should be designed accordingly before any dating is to be attempted. Even with specialized pretreatment, contamination cannot always be detected and if detected it cannot always be eliminated.

Despite the fact that all this is well known to archaeologists, what has stuck in the mind of the public is that the shroud dates to the Middle Ages and so it must be a fraud. It is true that if the carbon 14 date is accurate, it would negate all of the nearly 1000 tests that point to its authenticity. I believe that the accepted dates of 1262-1390 have another explanation consistent with every known characteristics of the cloth. This is referred to as the historically consistent method.

It is generally held that some form of radiant energy, electromagnetic or particle, is required to produce a three-dimensional digital encoded image. Even a recent production by the History Channel has stated as much by showing how the shroud is actually a digital map for producing a three-dimensional object. It is not a photo of Jesus; it is actually a code for making a three-dimensional model. The *Real Face of Jesus* (available from the History Channel), was produced from the digital data on the shroud and then the three-dimensional mold was subsequently reverse engineered back into a shroud like a print from a Xerox process!

The show's producers conceded to a mystical explanation but stopped short of giving it a Christian explanation. That is to be expected and I am grateful for the work they did. While a radiation type process now has a high level of acceptance, it does nothing to explain the dating problem, which still remains a potential defeater for a first century origin. Some researchers propose that the radiation that encoded the image was not electromagnetic in nature (light, ultraviolet, or x-ray), but consisted of protons and neutrons, the building blocks of matter.

This hypothesis has a wide scope and explanatory power. The source of the protons and neutrons would be the body itself. The vertical directionality of the features would come from the simple act of the cloth collapsing through the vacated space. Protons attenuate in about four centimeters of air, accounting for the darkening out of the image where the cloth is four centimeters from the body. If you picture a cloth draped over a mannequin and imagine the points of contact and the points of empty space, the points of contact will be where the image is most intense. Furthermore, protons are ionizing and will produce the straw yellow color by oxidation of the carbon-carbon double bonds.

Unlike protons, neutrons are not attenuated at short distances and would bounce all over the area like billiard balls, irradiating the whole shroud, including the walls of the tomb, to a depth of several feet. The neutrons will interact with nitrogen 14 in the air just over the cloth, producing a carbon 14 nucleus that would recoil into the cloth and become chemically bonded to the material itself. This additional carbon 14 would make the shroud appear younger than it actually is. But is this just a wild theory?

This particular nuclear reaction (N13 + n > C14) is well-known, but has not been studied on linen. These researchers have now radiated many samples of linen, both ancient and modern, with a standard dose of protons and neutrons in a research reactor, which produced the same degree of yellowing found in the shroud itself. The samples were then subjected to conditions to mimic the history of the shroud. This includes artificial aging and heating to duplicate the shroud's age and exposure to fire.

When these samples were sent to a radio-carbon dating lab, the results were astonishing. The age of the linen advanced by 1200 to 1400 years! This accounts for the C14 dating of a first century cloth to the Middle Ages. These tests provided a plausible mechanism for accounting for both the intensity of the image and the measured date of the cloth itself.

Antonacci and Lind presented these papers at a scientific conference on the shroud in Rome in 2010.[131] Subsequently, there has been greater acceptance of particle radiation as the basis for the unique characteristics of the shroud. Researchers have established not only a plausible mechanism to account for the date and the image we see, but also a basis for definitively testing this mechanism that would remove any doubt as to the source of the radiation. Additional tests could prove this beyond a reasonable doubt. If the particle radiation theory is true, signature isotopes (in addition to the added C14) such as Ca 41 and Cl 36 could, in principle, be found on shroud samples in amounts in excess of their background abundance. Researchers are currently attempting to do this but the technical difficulties are formidable.

I have added this additional information on the Shroud of Turin, not as a substitute for the biblical and historical case, but as an addition to the biblical witness. This evidence may appeal to a generation that is more oriented to the visual and scientific rather than the historical and the documentary evidence.

Jesus said that if you don't trust what the Old Testament prophets said about the coming Messiah, you will not believe even if one rose from the dead. If at this point you are not disposed to believe in the resurrection, it is doubtful that this evidence from the shroud will convince you. However, I've seen many people who are interested in the shroud that would not consider the Bible.

---

131 M. Antonacci and A.C. Lind, "Can Contamination Be Detected on the Turin Shroud" (Keynote paper, Turin, Italy, 2010).

Leading resurrection scholar Gary Habermas, who is circumspect in his pronouncements in these areas, has 80% confidence that the shroud is a record of the resurrection. I have spoken with a computer imaging specialist who puts that number as high as 98%. The scientific tools to investigate the shroud did not exist until recently. I think God made these tools available at just the right time for modern scientific skeptics. Unless someone comes up with a plausible naturalistic model accounting for all the shroud's features, the shroud stands as another brick in the cumulative case for the bodily resurrection of Jesus.

For more information go to: Resurrecting the Shroud Foundation at: www.resurrectionoftheshroud.com/About_Us.html

Appendix II. Is Hell as Hot as it Used To Be... or, What About the Lost?

● ● ●

The title of this book and the recurring theme of Pascal's wager imply that there are two sides and two outcomes entailed in how we choose to relate to God. Regardless of what metaphorical picture you have in mind concerning final outcomes, you all know that if God exists, your final status will be something to look forward to or something to be dreaded.

I want to clarify what I believe the Bible says about the negative side of the bet. You likely have been thinking about it (intentionally or not) from the moment the theme of the book became apparent. It is the elephant in the room whenever the Christian gospel—the good news—is presented. If the gospel is good news, then what exactly is the bad news?

The bad news, according to the traditional view, is some form of eternal conscious torment. In a culture that is loath to judge anyone for anything, the idea that a loving God would physically torture someone for all of eternity seems preposterous on the face of it. Very few churches include it in their preaching, even if they believe it. Evangelical leaders like Billy Graham preferred to use language like eternal separation from God.

Recently mega-church pastor Rob Bell put out a bestseller called *Love Wins*. In it he tries to make a case that some way, somehow, God eventually reconciles everyone to himself because God is love (1 John 4:8). Bell immediately became a media darling, making the rounds of the morning talk shows. Secular media are usually more than happy to promote someone from "inside the camp" that seems to be in opposition to anything they deem harsh, judgmental, or can be construed as fundamentalist.

However one eventually comes out on the issue, I don't think it should be based on Bell's work, which is devoid of sound reasoning or a careful exposition of scripture. Bell's position on most questions of doctrine is that the doctrine "is true–or not." Truth just does not seem to be a substantial category for Pastor Bell, hence his popularity with the postmodern generation. Bell's apologetic purpose may be to win people who have rejected Christianity because of their understanding of the doctrine of hell. To do this he advances three propositions in *Love Wins*: 1) Everyone is saved: God wants all to be saved; God gets what he wants. 2) Everyone is not saved. We can refuse God's love. 3) We don't know if everyone is saved on not. These statements are inconsistent with each other so they cannot all be true[132]. This is the kind of "truth decay" Bell finds works so well with a generation that hates absolutes. Bell also seems to neglect another attribute of God, his justice. The popularity of karma, an impersonal mechanistic form of justice the universe somehow dispenses, shows us that deep down, we want justice.

Bell's idea is called Universalism and it is a very attractive view. It was first taught by Origen in the third century but it didn't

---

132 Douglas Groothius, *What About Hell?* (lecture, Longmont, CO, 2012).

catch on due to a lack of support from tradition or scripture. It has become mainstream in many churches, not due to any careful philosophical or biblical analysis, but due to the spirit of the times, and for some understandable reasons. Surely we would wish that in the end that all, or at least most, would be saved. Certainly there is something wrong with our Christianity if we don't love people enough to hope that all would be saved. In fact, the Bible says that this is precisely what God would prefer.

According to the prophet Ezekiel, God has no pleasure in the death of the wicked, but only in their salvation. In the NT, Peter (2 Peter 3:9) writes that God does not want anyone to be destroyed. Surely we should feel the same way. But as we saw with the problem of evil, even omnipotence can't have all outcomes given free will. So Universalism fails, not because of some defect in God, but a defect in us. God will not drag the unwilling into his kingdom.

The philosophical basis for the traditional view is that any sin against an infinitely perfect being demands infinite punishment. If you remember back to the cosmological argument, any talk about infinity gets tricky really fast; I don't think this kind of reasoning is solid even though some Christian philosophers will make the argument. Christian philosophers, if they are to remain Christian, have to operate within the bounds of scripture.

Those holding the traditional view think they are teaching what the Bible says on the subject. The fact is that outside of scripture—that is, outside of God's revelation—there is no way of knowing about these eternal things at all. If scriptures don't guide us in theological matters we end up guided by our assumptions, traditions, or by our own preferences. As the apostle Paul would say, our thinking becomes futile.

People today seem to simply assume that their dead loved ones have somehow gone to heaven or to a better place, regardless of any faith they have held or how they may have lived. This kind of universalism is based on sentiment rather than on revelation or reason. There's a strong psychological reason that in the popular imagination all, or most people, go to heaven. Most people find it extremely difficult to imagine that God would send their love ones off to eternal punishment. But the other side of that line is that many people also find it extremely difficult to imagine that God might in the end forgive serial rapists and mass murderers or even their own personal enemies!

There are some biblical arguments that seem to support universalism. For example, in John 12:32, Jesus talks about drawing all people to himself, but just because Jesus/God wants to draw you to himself doesn't mean you will come, at least given a libertarian understanding of free will. But the same book says that those who have done evil will be condemned (John 5:29) and that those who disobey the son of God will remain under God's punishment (John 3:36). In Philippians 2:10, Paul writes that all beings that inhabit the earth and under the earth (the dead) will proclaim that Jesus is Lord. But it's clear that even the demons recognize that Jesus is Lord so this is not an argument for reconciliation. And then a bit later in Philippians 3:19, Paul also says that's there are some people whose end is destruction.

It is clear that only when you take a few texts out of context that you can possibly claim that the Bible teaches universalism.

Another attempt at universalism comes out of a misplaced idea of God's sovereignty. The assumption is that God doesn't want any to perish (2 Peter 3:9) and somewhere the scripture says God always accomplishes his will. The problem here in using these verses as a proof for universalism is that they are not connected. By this method you can make them say anything. Peter is saying the reason for God's apparent slowness to come in judgment is that God wants to give this generation (of Jews) time to repent. There is no possible interpretation here that would support universalism.

So what does the Bible actually say? Jesus spends more time talking about hell than heaven. But what exactly does the word mean? In Mathew 25:40, Jesus tells of the fate of those who neglect "The least of these" meaning the poor and down trodden. He says they will go to eternal punishment, but the righteous will go into eternal life. The place he points to as hell is Gehenna, an actual place in the Valley of Hinnom where in Old Testament times Pagans would sacrifice their children to the god Molach.

In Jesus' time, Gehenna was the Jerusalem city dump where the trash fires were kept burning. By analogy, evil people similarly would be taken to the city dump to be disposed of or destroyed. More justification for the ultimate destruction of the wicked is Matthew 10:28 "Fear only God, who can destroy both soul and body in hell." Body and soul is a reference to the whole person. This teaches that our destruction will be complete. Other verses continue with the theme that the lost will be separated out like the wheat from the chaff and thrown into the fire for complete burning.

The Bible is consistent in insisting that some will be lost forever. As Paul says in 2 Thessalonians 1:9, "They will be punished with everlasting destruction, forever separated from the Lord and from his glorious power." Whatever else the word "everlasting" means here, it certainly means that there will be no comeback; whatever else the word "destruction" means it certainly does not mean salvation.

So why has the eternal conscious torment prevailed in Church history? One reason is confusion over the flames being eternal as opposed to our time spent in the flames being eternal. Readers have simply made the assumption that our time in the fire is the same as the extent of the fire. A second point is that while Jesus meant for hell to be very real, he spoke about it in metaphorical language. His use of Gehenna, the city dump, was something he could point to that everyone understood. Jesus says it would be better to get rid of whatever causes sin than "...be thrown into hell where the worm never dies and the fire never goes out" (Mark 9:48). Is using the words from Isaiah 66:24, "And as they go out they will see the dead bodies of those who have rebelled against me. For the worms that devour them will never die and the fire that burns them will never go out. All who pass by will view them with utter horror." These words have formed the basis for much Christian teaching on hell ever since. But it is important to go look at what they actually say. The righteous "go out and look" on their enemies' corpses, not on living people. They view their destruction, not their misery. To burn a corpse signified a thing utterly accursed or marked for God's destruction. This was the Jewish view. This is what Jesus was communicating. The Jewish apostle Peter draws this same conclusion: "(God) turned the cities of Sodom and Gomorrah into heaps of ashes and swept them off the face of the earth. He made them an example of what will happen to ungodly people" (2 Peter 2:6).

No doubt it will be terrible for the lost on the Day of Judgment, but the traditional notion of eternal torture is not found in these verses. If not here, where else is it more clear?

We know the flame language is metaphorical because hell is also referred to as a place of outer darkness. This is clearly inconsistent with flames. Another difficulty is confusing eternal punishment with eternal punishing. When someone is executed they are dead forever, so the punishment is eternal. However the punishing only goes on for a time. Perhaps the strongest argument the proponents of eternal conscious torment make is that heaven is described as an eternal reward, so hell must be an eternal punishment. But these ideas are not necessarily symmetrical. As we have just seen, the idea of an eternal punishment can refer to a state of death, but living eternally can refer to a state of life. John 3:16 may be the strongest verse of all that teaches eternal life is conditional on belief in Jesus: "Whoever believes in him shall not perish but have eternal life." The passage goes on to say that those who do not believe in God the son will perish and not have eternal life. There is no language connected to this part of scripture that says those that do not believe in Jesus will go on to eternal anything.

I think conditional immortality has something to say to those attracted to Eastern religion. Though they belong to two different metaphysical systems, both of which cannot be true, I find it curious that the Christian hell, the second death in the lake of fire, and the Eastern view of extinction of the self, amount to the same effective outcome. The Eastern view celebrates this escape while the biblical view sees this as a tragic loss.

The job description of Satan, the father of lies, is to reverse everything (For an interesting take on this, read C. S. Lewis' book *The Screwtape Letters*, in which the demons work to reverse everything). The Bible urges us to choose life. Satan urges us to choose death, whether through abortion, war, euthanasia, and ultimately by rejecting Christ. This coincidence of outcomes should give one pause as to who they are following down the path to nirvana. Eastern religion and all its variants: the New Age, nature worship, Wicca, and other neo-Pagan practices all are deceptions that lead to the same end.

I believe conditional immortality has far more biblical support than either universalism or eternal conscious torment. Besides being biblical, it has several advantages in communicating God is not unjust. Eternal conscious torment offends people's sensibilities. By now you should know that I care about what God says and not people's sensibilities; but why make it worse than it is by adding to "the offense of the gospel"? On the other hand universalism should be equally offensive with worst-case offenders who spend a life of rebellion against God getting a free pass. Least one think that the conditional view somehow diminishes God's justice, I believe it is in conformity with God's justice. The Old Testament penalty of an eye for an eye seem harsh to us now, but when it was introduced by

God through Moses into the ancient Near East, it brought the idea of proportional punishment to a culture that demanded extreme penalties for the slightest offense. The conditionalist view allows for God's justice where one has to give an account for, and pay a proportional penalty for one's sins. The conditionalist view gives no time marker as to how long this might take or the exact nature of the penalty. But the Bible assures us: Should not the judge of all the earth do what is right? (Genesis 18:25). For those who do not believe in Christ, what is *not* fair about them *not* inheriting eternal life? Revelation 20:13 says that "They were all judged according to their deeds. And death and the grave were thrown into the lake of fire. This is the second death." I don't see how one could object to proportional punishment. Our sense of justice demands it. I also do not see how anyone could say God owes them immortality, especially to those who are just not interested, as many of my friends tell me they are not.

To the Traditionalists who would argue I just overlooked Revelation 20:10, where the devil and the false prophet are tormented "forever and ever," I remind them that the book of Revelation is of the apocalyptic genre. (It is also called the Apocalypse of John). One of the characteristics of this genre is to globalize local events and eternalize temporal events. Biblical writers often used the language of this genre to make a point. When Paul said he preached the gospel "to the whole world" he meant his world, the Roman world. When Genesis speaks of the flood covering the whole earth, it need not mean any more than the immediate surroundings. This was all worked out in Milton Terry's books *Biblical Apocalyptic*, and

Biblical Hermeneutics one hundred years ago. The word studies are compelling and solve a host of Bible difficulties.

The idea of the immortality of the soul actually comes from Greek philosophy and is not inherently a Jewish or Christian idea. It is also found in Plato, Eastern religion, and the un-biblical idea of reincarnation. The Bible says, "...as it is destined that each person dies once and after that comes judgment..." The early Church, set in a Greek world, found a certain utility in some ideas from Greek philosophy, some of which stuck and are not necessarily biblical.

Some advocates of the traditional view think that by backing off from it we may lessen the seriousness of the need for salvation by Christ's sacrifice. But I remind people the Bible gives a clear and consistent message that those who knowingly reject the salvation offered through the gift of grace will regret it. There is a good and a bad outcome, life or death, and the Bible says, "choose life."

Made in the USA
Charleston, SC
01 May 2013